Name_____

What kind of ears do engines have?

1. her aunt
2. a green dress
3. Grandfather
4. the small tree
5. a red car
6. everybody
7. a blue lake
8. the horse trainer
9. strawberries

	who	what
1.	(e)	b
2.	c	n
3.	g	d
4.	f	i
5.	g	n
6.	e	h
7.	i	e
8.	r	j
9.	k	s

© Frank Schaffer Publications, Inc. FS-32032 Reading Activities

Name_____

1. new shoes
2. a truck driver
3. a buzzing bee
4. the farmer
5. falling snow
6. Jerry
7. Linda
8. the toy train
9. tree branches
10. Mr. Green
11. yellow sunlight
12. the little house

	who	what
1.	s	(a)
2.	b	r
3.	t	a
4.	c	r
5.	v	k
6.	w	d
7.	a	o
8.	m	r
9.	n	d
10.	b	p
11.	l	e
12.	s	e

© Frank Schaffer Publications, Inc.   FS-32032 Reading Activities

Name_____

What do giraffes have that no other animal has?

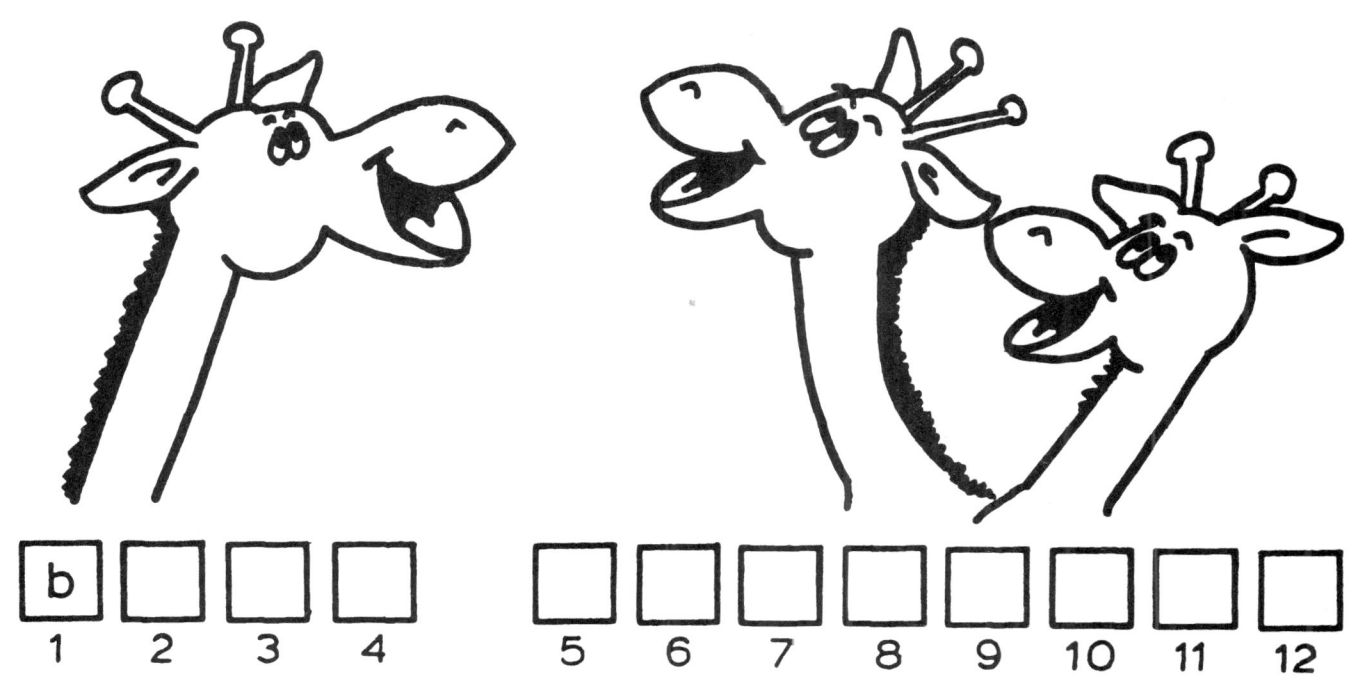

	1	2	3	4		5	6	7	8	9	10	11	12
	b												

		who	when
1. a big girl	1.	(b)	y
2. tomorrow	2.	r	a
3. two years ago	3.	g	b
4. four boys	4.	y	f
5. after dinner	5.	a	g
6. Judy and Susan	6.	i	m
7. his brother	7.	r	o
8. last week	8.	t	a
9. later on	9.	e	f
10. her family	10.	f	r
11. today	11.	s	e
12. Mr. James	12.	s	f

Name_____

What is the smallest room in the world?

This one is quite small.

	1	2	3	4	5	6	7	8	9
	a								

1. his brother
2. my classmates
3. on the lake
4. in the sky
5. a busdriver
6. under the table
7. two friends
8. inside the box
9. a tall boy

	who	where
1.	ⓐ	t
2.	m	a
3.	l	u
4.	p	s
5.	h	o
6.	e	r
7.	o	u
8.	a	o
9.	m	k

Name_____

What two animals go everywhere you go?

1. in a little while
2. behind that book
3. next summer
4. over the barn
5. in the evening
6. into the water
7. after dark
8. on the top step
9. the last day
10. down the hill

	where		when
1.	w	1.	(y)
2.	o	2.	x
3.	p	3.	u
4.	r	4.	s
5.	t	5.	c
6.	a	6.	d
7.	f	7.	l
8.	v	8.	g
9.	m	9.	e
10.	s	10.	n

Name _____

What does a duck do when he flies upside down?

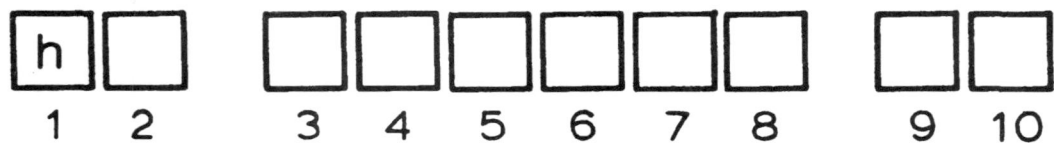

1. airplanes
2. an apple tree
3. in the morning
4. a field of hay
5. at sunset
6. next week
7. a yellow basket
8. never again
9. at noon
10. closed the gate

	what	when
1.	(h)	g
2.	e	f
3.	d	q
4.	u	v
5.	x	a
6.	m	c
7.	k	n
8.	r	s
9.	t	u
10.	p	w

Name_____

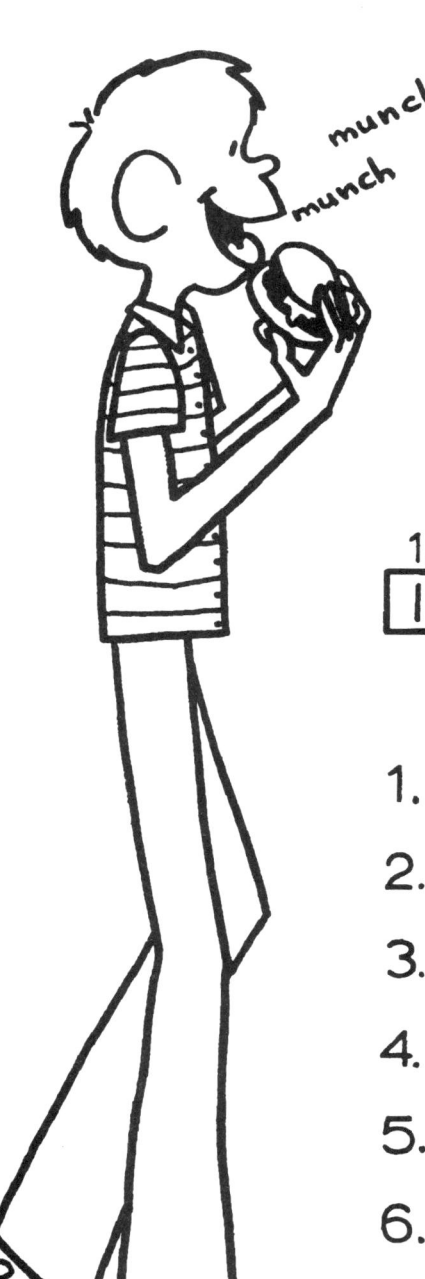

If hamburgers grew on trees, what would they be called?

1. 2. 3. 4. 5. 6. 7. 8. 9. 10.
[l] [ ] [ ] [ ] [ ] [ ] [ ] [ ] [ ] [ ]

where-what

1. in a field   1. (l) (m)
2. inside the house   2. (i) (j)
3. a new shoe   3. (s) (m)
4. one shiny saw   4. (r) (b)
5. outside the store 5. (u) (v)
6. the oak tree   6. (t) (r)
7. her blue coat   7. (o) (g)
8. in the lake   8. (e) (f)
9. on the hill   9. (r) (g)
10. a red truck   10. (q) (s)

Name_____

What grows down instead of up?

a ◯ ◯ ◯ ◯ ◯
1. 2. 3. 4. 5. 6.

                            when   why

1. to go up that road   1. | c | a |
2. in a little while   2. | g | h |
3. for the sun was bright   3. | a | o |
4. once upon a time   4. | o | f |
5. to close the door   5. | i | s |
6. on the first day   6. | e | l |

Name_____

How many skunks does it take to smell up a neighborhood?

j								
1	2	3	4	5	6	7	8	9

                          where why

1. for the stairs are dark   1. (m) (j)
2. over the barn   2. (u) (b)
3. because the sun set   3. (e) (s)
4. beside the gate   4. (t) (s)
5. in order to swim   5. (f) (a)
6. to get to their car   6. (o) (p)
7. on top of the table   7. (h) (m)
8. into the room   8. (e) (l)
9. because he was happy   9. (o) (w)

Name_____

What can go over the water and through the water without getting wet?

1. 2. 3. 4. 5. 6. 7. 8.

what how

1. opened the door   1. (s) o
2. running swiftly   2. (m) u
3. pulled a rope   3. (n) a
4. green clover   4. (l) t
5. slower and slower   5. (c) i
6. yellow flowers   6. (g) f
7. turning quickly   7. (o) h
8. climbing boldly   8. (b) t

Name_____

What country do fish come from?

1. in the woods
2. coming slowly
3. turning and twisting
4. on the shelf
5. under the floor
6. kicking and splashing
7. cutting neatly
8. in his pocket
9. shining brightly
10. in a stream
11. over the shed

	how	where
1.	m	(f)
2.	r	b
3.	o	t
4.	d	m
5.	o	f
6.	i	g
7.	n	h
8.	s	l
9.	a	t
10.	u	n
11.	p	d

Name_____

What is the difference between an old dime and a new nickel?

```
[f][ ][ ][ ]   [ ][ ][ ][ ][ ]
 1. 2. 3. 4.    5. 6. 7. 8. 9.
```

                          who what when

1. two new shoes   1. (d) (f) (g)
2. in the morning   2. (c) (h) (i)
3. his birthday cake   3. (o) (v) (t)
4. the horse trainer   4. (e) (m) (s)
5. at ten o'clock   5. (l) (d) (c)
6. a carpenter   6. (e) (t) (a)
7. before breakfast   7. (b) (o) (n)
8. her grandfather   8. (t) (x) (y)
9. the big brown chair   9. (z) (s) (u)

Name _____

What is the smallest bridge in the world?

The bridge
1. 2. 3. 4. 5. 6. 7. 8. 9. 10.

what when where

1. a buzzing bee   1. (o) (a) (i)
2. before the rain   2. (g) (f) (h)
3. in a little while   3. (x) (y) (z)
4. under the log   4. (m) (n) (o)
5. the blue lake   5. (u) (s) (t)
6. over the trees   6. (q) (d) (r)
7. on the boat   7. (p) (l) (n)
8. a green coat   8. (o) (r) (t)
9. after sunset   9. (u) (s) (v)
10. thunder clouds   10. (e) (w) (x)

Name_____

What two keys are too big to carry in your pocket?

"It depends on the pocket!"

m ◯ ◯ — ◯ ◯ ◯ and ◯ ◯ ◯ — ◯ ◯ ◯
1. 2. 3. 4. 5. 6.   7. 8. 9. 10. 11. 12.

	when	where	why
1. on Monday afternoon — 1.	(m)	n	o
2. asked him to come — 2.	p	q	o
3. behind her chair — 3.	r	n	s
4. all that day — 4.	k	l	h
5. around the house — 5.	f	e	g
6. to open that box — 6.	w	x	y
7. because the wind blew — 7.	b	c	d
8. under all the sand — 8.	r	o	s
9. late that night — 9.	n	u	x
10. in a far off time — 10.	k	h	j
11. high in a tree — 11.	g	e	m
12. for the wind was cold — 12.	n	s	y

© Frank Schaffer Publications, Inc.

What is bought by the yard and worn by the foot?

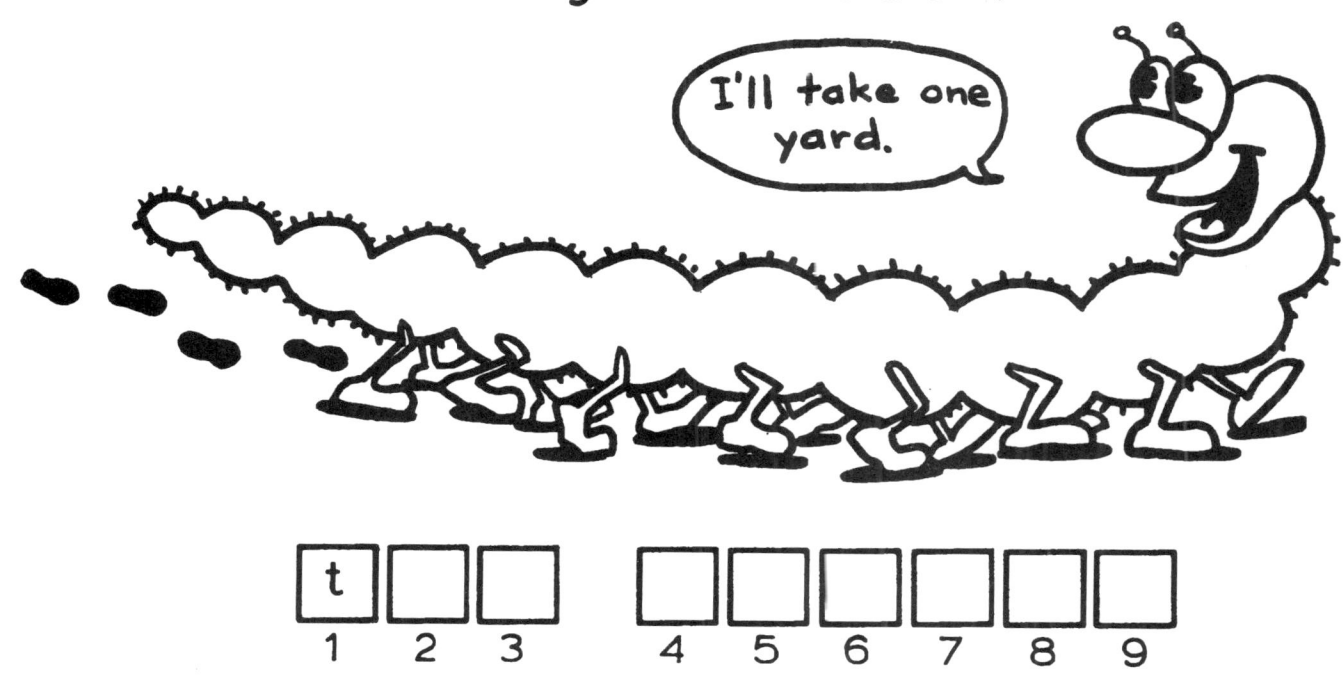

"I'll take one yard."

t								
1	2	3	4	5	6	7	8	9

	where	why	how
1. because he was happy	r	(t)	s
2. on the roof	h	g	k
3. jumped quickly	f	a	e
4. because the storm came	b	c	d
5. climbing carefully	l	m	a
6. under the hill	r	u	y
7. he slid to a stop	x	n	p
8. for they were lost	j	e	u
9. in the bookshelf	t	z	m

Name_____

"...but I like spots!"

What's another name for a spot remover?

A [d] [ ] [ ] [ ] [ ] [ ] [ ] [ ] [ ] [ ]
   1. 2. 3. 4. 5. 6. 7. 8. 9. 10.

who what when where

1. strawberries   1. (c) (d) (e) (f)
2. by the door   2. (m) (n) (p) (o)
3. four girls   3. (g) (h) (k) (l)
4. yesterday   4. (a) (b) (c) (d)
5. his uncle   5. (a) (f) (t) (u)
6. a green basket   6. (q) (t) (r) (s)
7. to the store   7. (u) (v) (w) (c)
8. on the floor   8. (x) (y) (n) (h)
9. in April   9. (h) (o) (e) (l)
10. his brother   10. (r) (k) (g) (h)

Name_____

When is a ship like snow?

When ⓘ ▢ ▢ ▢ - ▢ ▢ ▢ ▢ ▢
     1   2   3   4   5   6   7   8   9

1. up the stairs
2. asked him to come
3. before the show
4. the biggest tree
5. into the cave
6. last winter
7. that red bird
8. in order to stop
9. the brown table

	what	when	where	why
1.	l	m	ⓘ	d
2.	a	d	b	t
3.	g	s	k	i
4.	a	p	t	r
5.	l	o	d	f
6.	k	r	j	e
7.	i	p	s	t
8.	b	g	h	f
9.	t	m	n	u

Name _____

What is the biggest ant in the world?

```
 1  2  3      4  5   6  7  8
(t)( )( )    ( )( )-( )( )( )
```

	when	where	why	how
1.	w	d	f	(t)
2.	h	j	k	l
3.	m	e	n	o
4.	p	q	g	r
5.	i	s	t	u
6.	v	w	x	a
7.	b	c	n	d
8.	t	e	f	g

1. singing loudly
2. yesterday
3. in the desk
4. for the top was big
5. before she came
6. very slowly
7. because they grew
8. never again

Name _____

Who is always happy when things go wrong?

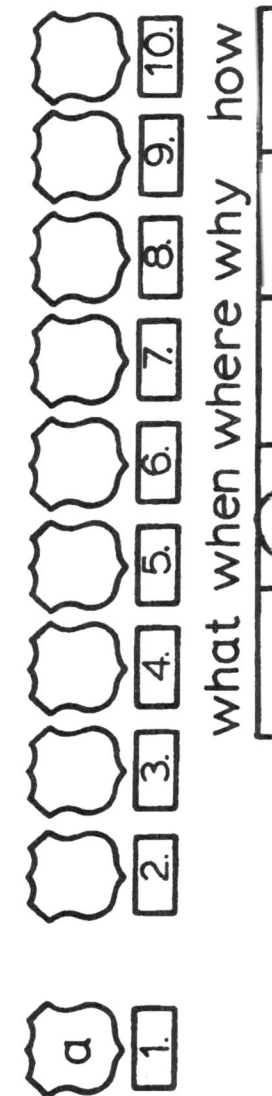

	what	when	where	why	how
1.	e	(a)	i	o	u
2.	g	h	r	s	t
3.	e	m	b	d	f
4.	n	q	r	p	s
5.	u	e	i	o	a
6.	f	i	q	u	e
7.	l	d	g	r	b
8.	k	h	j	p	m
9.	h	o	a	m	l
10.	n	r	s	t	u

1. late tomorrow
2. beside the river
3. the red kite
4. to open the door
5. laughing merrily
6. someday soon
7. because he cared
8. slower and slower
9. down in the water
10. the red berries

a 1. 2. 3. 4. 5. 6. 7. 8. 9. 10.

© Frank Schaffer Publications, Inc.   FS-32032 Reading Activities

Name _____

What is a raisin?

"Yummy!"

wo ⓡ ◯ ◯ ◯ ◯ ◯ ◯ ◯ ◯ ◯
1. 2. 3. 4. 5. 6. 7. 8. 9. 10.

	who	what	when	where	why	how
1.	s	ⓡ	t	u	v	w
2.	r	m	b	d	l	g
3.	a	e	i	o	u	y
4.	v	r	g	d	e	f
5.	s	u	m	d	y	z
6.	l	m	n	p	q	g
7.	a	r	b	c	d	h
8.	a	f	t	r	p	n
9.	o	n	p	r	l	v	r
10.	c	k	l	e	u	y

1. a birthday cake
2. a bus driver
3. the next day
4. in order to do it
5. outside the store
6. turning slowly
7. a big red apple
8. the bike rider
9. once upon a time
10. under the tree

Name _____ Skill: Compound words

Finish the compound word under each picture.
Write the words in ABC order.

Word Box

snake	berry
hook	cup
corn	fly
rise	bow
plane	nail

ABC Order

1. tea
2. butter
3. rattle
4. fish
5. rain
6. air
7. pop
8. straw
9. finger
10. sun

Name _____ Skill: Compound words

Match the words to make compound words.
Write the compound words.

hand	mother	handshake
news	cat	
wild	shake	
grand	boat	
row	paper	
under	boat	
sail	cake	
pan	water	
flower	head	
fore	pot	
fish	meal	
day	light	
road	net	
oat	side	
some	body	

Name _____ Skill: **Compound words**

Use a word from **Word Box 1** and a word from **Word Box 2** to make a compound word for each meaning. Write the compound word.

1. something to drink   _____
2. an animal   _____
3. an insect   _____
4. a direction   _____
5. place for dishes   _____
6. a meal   _____
7. behind house   _____
8. for letters   _____
9. for plants   _____
10. where you sleep   _____

Word Box 1		Word Box 2	
cup	flower	shake	room
milk	back	cat	board
bed	butter	fly	fast
north	mail	east	yard
wild	break	pot	box

Name _____ Skill: Plurals **s**, **es**

Add **s** or **es** to make each word a plural.
Add **es** if the word ends with **sh**, **ch**, **x** or **s**.
Write the word on the line.

carrot _____	tiger _____
beach _____	sock _____
shoe _____	farm _____
dress _____	seal _____
ranch _____	park _____
dog _____	fox _____
lunch _____	watch _____
peach _____	apple _____

Write the plural words in the correct place on the chart.

Animals	Things to Eat	Places	Things to Wear

Name _____   Skill: Plurals **ies, ves**

Change each word to the plural form. Write the word on the line.
Change **f** to **v** and add **es**.
Change **y** to **i** and add **es**.

1. The _____ are pretty colors.
                   leaf

2. We picked _____ in the woods.
                        berry

3. We saw a movie about _____.
                                   wolf

4. The _____ are in the barn.
                   calf

5. There are two _____ in the city.
                           library

6. Dad built _____ in the garage.
                       shelf

7. It costs a dollar to ride the _____.
                                       pony

8. The story is about seven tiny _____.
                                       elf

9. _____ are fun to watch at night.
      Firefly

10. Mother planted _____ in the yard.
                           lily

11. The mother lion has three _____.
                                       baby

12. The police caught the _____.
                                    thief

Name _____   Skill: Plurals **s**, **es**, **ies**, **ves**

Change each word to the plural form. Write the word on the line.

1. The _____ are hiding in the _____ .
     squirrel   ditch

2. You will see _____ at many _____ .
               seal   beach

3. Put the _____ in the _____ .
           firefly   jar

4. How many _____ did you pick from the _____ ?
            berry   bush

5. Put the _____ in the _____ .
           letter   mailbox

6. Put the _____ on the _____ .
           brush   shelf

7. I bought two _____ for my _____ .
                watch   friend

8. We saw ten _____ on three _____ .
              bird   branch

9. I want two _____ for my _____ .
              lollipop   sister

10. The _____ are taking their _____ .
        baby   nap

© Frank Schaffer Publications, Inc.   FS-32032 Reading Activities

Name _____   Skill: Contractions

Write the contraction.

1. do | not _____
2. I | will _____
3. it | is _____
4. will | not _____
5. could | not _____
6. they | are _____
7. we | are _____
8. she | is _____
9. we | will _____
10. does | not _____
11. who | is _____
12. has | not _____
13. you | are _____
14. I | am _____
15. should | not _____

Name _____   Skill: Contractions

Circle the missing words. Make them into a contraction.
Write the contraction on the line.

1. We _____ expecting a big crowd.
       did not   were not

2. Next time _____ come early!
       I will   I am

3. We _____ seen this movie.
       do not   have not

4. I know _____ like it.
       you will   he is

5. This movie _____ for adults.
       can not   is not

6. This line _____ moved.
       has not   we are

7. I _____ want to be last in line!
       is not   would not

8. _____ open soon.
       I am   They will

9. I _____ bring my bubble gum.
       do not   did not

10. _____ worry, we will get seats.
        Could not   Do not

11. Look, _____ selling tickets now.
        we were   they are

12. Ouch, _____ standing on my toe!
        you are   I am

Name _____   Skill: Possessives, Contractions for **is**

Sam's dog is big.   (**'s** shows possession)
Sam's late today.   (**'s** shows a contraction for **is**)

Make a ✓ to show what **'s** stands for.

	possession	**is**
1. Sam's late today.		✓
2. Where is Mike's house?		
3. Kim's going to camp.		
4. Is that Jane's kitten?		
5. Mother's going to be here soon.		
6. The newspaper's late today.		
7. Put the teacher's papers on his desk.		
8. Show me the baby's room.		
9. Dad's car won't start!		
10. The bell's going to ring.		
11. Today is Matt's birthday.		
12. The door's unlocked.		
13. Where is the dog's bone?		
14. The baby's sleeping now.		
15. The puppy's hungry.		

Write a sentence using **'s** to show possession.

_____

Write a sentence using **'s** as a contraction for **is**.

_____

29

Name _____ Skill: **Possessives**

Fill in the missing words.

"Meet our family"
"Toto is my dog"
"My cat is named Silky."

| Mr. Bumble | Mrs. Bumble | Scott | Toto | Sara | Silky |

1. Sara is _____ sister.

2. Toto is _____ dog.

3. Mrs. Bumble is _____ wife.

4. Scott is _____ brother.

5. _____ cat is named Silky.

6. Mr. Bumble is _____ husband.

7. Scott and Sara are Mr. and Mrs. _____ children.

8. Mr. and Mrs. Bumble are Scott and _____ parents.

Name _____   Skill: **Synonyms**

Circle a synonym for the underlined word.
Write another synonym from the **Word Box** on the line.

1. intelligent   bright   friendly   _____
2. assist   repair   aid   _____
3. frigid   chilly   weather   _____
4. puzzled   mean   baffled   _____
5. bravery   boldness   frighten   _____
6. dangerous   huge   hazardous   _____
7. easy   careful   uncomplicated   _____
8. trade   exchange   buy   _____
9. repair   sell   mend   _____
10. happiness   joy   smile   _____
11. calm   quiet   pretty   _____
12. power   loud   strength   _____

Word Box

- gladness
- courage
- simple
- help
- risky
- confused
- fix
- swap
- smart
- force
- cold
- peace

Name _____ Skill: Synonyms

Selecting Synonyms

Words that have about the same meaning, like *choose* and *pick* are called **synonyms**.

Circle the synonyms for the first word in each row.

1. fast | quick   hard   swift   speedy   small
2. bright | dazzling   dull   glittering   sparkling
3. friend | stranger   companion   chum   pal   buddy
4. scary | scream   frightening   rough   terrifying
5. throw | fling   carry   hurl   toss   catch

Look at each picture below. Using the words you circled, write a list of synonyms to describe each picture.

1. _fast_

2. _bright_

3. _friend_

4. _scary_

5. _throw_

Brainwork! Make a list of at least five synonyms for *look*.

Name _____   Skill: Synonyms

Substituting Synonyms

Words that have about the same meaning, like *substitute* and *replace*, are called **synonyms**.

Choose the word from the Word Box that could replace the boldfaced word in each sentence. Write the word on the line. Use a dictionary to help you with new words.

Word Box

fortunate	grimy
torrid	select
discovered	ancient
entire	chuckle

1. The dinosaur bones were **old**.
_____

2. We were **lucky** that it didn't rain.
_____

3. After playing football, my clothes were **dirty**.
_____

4. That joke made me **laugh**.
_____

5. I rode my bike the **whole** way home.
_____

6. I had to **choose** a book for my report.
_____

7. It was a **hot** day in the desert.
_____

8. I **found** the missing puzzle piece on the floor.
_____

Brainwork! Rewrite this sentence substituting synonyms for the boldfaced words: The **lucky** scientists **found** some **old** bones.

Name _____ **Skill: Antonyms**

Write an antonym for the underlined words.
Use words from the **Word Box**.

1. a <u>sad</u> story _____
2. a <u>tiny</u> dinosaur _____
3. an <u>ugly</u> butterfly _____
4. a <u>sweet</u> lemon _____
5. a <u>short</u> skyscraper _____
6. a <u>soft</u> rock _____
7. a <u>cold</u> dog _____
8. a <u>thin</u> hippo _____
9. <u>dirty</u> hands _____
10. the <u>dim</u> sun _____
11. a <u>laughing</u> baby _____
12. a <u>light</u> suitcase _____
13. a <u>start</u> sign _____
14. a <u>slow</u> race _____
15. a big <u>frown</u> _____

Word Box

- tall
- pretty
- hot
- bright
- stop
- happy
- crying
- hard
- fast
- heavy
- huge
- smile
- fat
- clean
- sour

Name _____ Skill: Antonyms

Write a word that means the opposite in the puzzle. Use the words in the Word Box.

Word Box

Across →
- 1. close
- 3. under
- 5. short
- 7. bottom
- 9. cry
- 11. difficult
- 13. bad

Down ↓
- 2. yes
- 4. left
- 6. found
- 8. push
- 10. love
- 12. old
- 14. wet

Name _____ Skill: Antonyms

Antonyms Are Opposites

Circle the pair of antonyms in each box. Complete each sentence with one of the circled words.

A. | sweet   quiet   noisy   fast |

1. The blowing horns were _____ .
2. It was _____ in the library.

B. | rough   empty   smooth   straight |

1. The cat's fur felt _____ .
2. The sandpaper was _____ .

C. | close   wrong   near   right |

1. Never drive the _____ way on a one-way street.
2. I got a prize for having the _____ answer.

D. | bought   decorated   sent   sold |

1. I _____ my old bike when I outgrew it.
2. Mom _____ me a warmer jacket.

E. | laugh   sleepy   lose   find |

1. Did you _____ the key I lost?
2. In a strange place, it's easy to _____ your way.

F. | break   own   hurt   repair |

1. A flying ball might _____ a window.
2. He needed tools to _____ the car.

G. | worn   neat   messy   quick |

1. I had to clean my _____ desk.
2. I like my handwriting to look _____ .

Brainwork! List at least five more antonym pairs.

© Frank Schaffer Publications, Inc.   37   FS-32032 Reading Activities

Name _____ Skill: Antonyms

Trading Places

Antonyms are words that have opposite meanings.

In each sentence below, circle the incorrect word. Then write the sentence replacing the circled word with its antonym from the Word Box. The first one has been done for you.

Word Box			
huge	dangerous	exit	drenched
future	better	raw	frown

1. The elephant was (tiny).
   The elephant was huge.

2. It is safe to touch electric wires.
   _____

3. After the rain the ground was dry.
   _____

4. A cooked carrot is hard and crunchy.
   _____

5. This medicine should make you feel worse.
   _____

6. The overdue book notice made me smile.
   _____

7. In the past I plan to go to college.
   _____

8. Go out through the entrance.
   _____

Brainwork! Write each of these words and its opposite: *seldom, forbid, succeed, apart, lend.*

Name _____ Skill: Synonyms/Antonyms

Circle two words that have almost the same meaning.

1. mistake   error   repair
2. rich   money   wealthy
3. frighten   startle   secret
4. song   noisy   loud
5. imitate   copy   return
6. hasty   funny   speedy

Circle two words that have opposite meanings.

1. cheap   expensive silly
2. watch   break   repair
3. travel   play   work
4. lost   found   cook
5. write   buy   sell
6. kind   friend   mean

Name _____   Skill: Synonyms/Antonyms

Write a synonym or antonym on the line. Use words from the **Word Box**.

Word Box
old	select
big	cute
play	wild
female	hard
tell	loves
baby	friend
found	long

Dear Pen Pal,

   I have something exciting to _____ you!
   ask (antonym)

Yesterday we went to the animal shelter. I

_____ three
lost (antonym)

kittens that were

_____ . It was _____ to decide which one
adorable (synonym)   _difficult (synonym)_

to _____ . I chose a _____ kitten. She is
  choose (synonym)   _male (antonym)_

six weeks _____ . She has _____ white fur
          young (antonym)   _short (antonym)_

with a _____ black spot on her face. She
       large (synonym)

_____ to _____ with a tissue on a string.
hates (antonym)   _work (antonym)_

She acts like a _____ tiger. We made a cozy bed for
                fierce (synonym)

her in a box. My _____ sister gave her a warm blanket
                 adult (antonym)

for her box. I'll send you a picture of my cat soon. Do you have

any pets?

                    Your _____ ,
                         pal (synonym)

    _____

Name _____ Skill: Synonyms and antonyms

Keep Track

Each clue for this puzzle asks for a synonym or an antonym for a word. The words you need are in the Word Box. To keep track of the difference between synonyms and antonyms, check the footprints by the puzzle.

Word Box

CHUCKLE	ELECT	FULL	ARRIVE
CAUTIOUS	BORROW	DREAD	HINDER
REPAIR	EXIT	LESS	EVEN

Across
2. antonym for odd
6. antonym for depart
8. synonym for careful
9. synonym for fear
10. antonym for empty
11. synonym for fix

Down
1. antonym for lend
2. antonym for enter
3. synonym for choose
4. synonym for fewer
5. synonym for laugh
7. antonym for help

Brainwork! Choose five of the words from the puzzle. Write sentences using those words.

Name _____ Skill: Homonyms

Handy Homonyms

Words that sound **the same** but have different spellings and meanings are called **homonyms**. Use the picture clues to help you choose the correct word for each sentence. Fill in the O above the word and write it on the line.

1. I got a letter in the _____ .
   ○ male ○ mail

2. The dog's _____ made muddy prints.
   ○ paws ○ pause

3. She was gone for an _____ .
   ○ hour ○ our

4. My favorite _____ is a rose.
   ○ flower ○ flour

5. Buy now and save ten _____ .
   ○ scents ○ cents

6. We chopped _____ for a fire.
   ○ would ○ wood

7. He hung the _____ to dry.
   ○ close ○ clothes

8. We nailed the _____ in place.
   ○ board ○ bored

9. I can _____ my name in cursive.
   ○ right ○ write

10. The _____ will be sunny.
    ○ weather ○ whether

11. Our team _____ the pennant.
    ○ won ○ one

12. I like to read _____ .
    ○ allowed ○ aloud

Brainwork! Write sentences to show the meanings of the unused words from five of the boxes above.

Name _____   Skill: Homonyms

In the Bag

Homonyms are words that sound alike but have different spellings and meanings.

Word Box							
know	for	threw	sale	flour	rolls	isle	pairs
no	four	through	sail	flower	roles	aisle	pears
by	one	cereal	beats	weekly	steak	There	so
buy	won	serial	beets	weakly	stake	Their	sew

Look at the pairs of homonyms in the Word Box. Read the story below and circle each incorrect word. Then rewrite the story using the correct words.

In the Bag

It was time four the weakly grocery shopping. Dad takes me because I no a good by when I see won. We walked threw every isle looking for what was on sail. Their were specials on stake, serial, pairs, flower, beats, and roles, sew we stocked up!

_____

_____
_____
_____
_____
_____
_____

Brainwork! Write a story that includes ten words from the Word Box. Be sure to choose the correct homonym for the meaning in your story.

Name _____   Skill: Homographs

Write a homograph that fits both clues.

Homographs

nail	well
limb	earth
deck	saw
safe	bill
star	bat

1. where we live / the soil
2. branch of a tree / arm or leg
3. not sick / deep hole with water
4. part of a bird's mouth / something you pay
5. part of a ship / group of cards
6. used to cut wood / had seen something
7. not risky / place to keep money
8. in the sky / a famous person
9. on your finger / hit with a hammer
10. for hitting a ball / lives in caves

© Frank Schaffer Publications, Inc.   44   FS-32032 Reading Activities

Name _____   Skill: Homophones

Write the correct word under each picture.

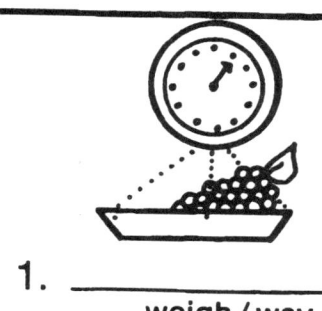
1. _____
weigh / way

2. _____
son / sun

3. _____
dough / doe

4. _____
flower / flour

5. _____
cheap / cheep

6. _____
stake / steak

7. _____
ate / eight

8. _____
sale / sail

9. _____
male / mail

10. _____
sew / so

11. _____
bare / bear

12. _____
sea / see

13. _____
pare / pear / pair

14. _____
pare / pear / pair

15. _____
pare / pear / pair

Name _____ Skill: Homophones

Write the missing word in each sentence.

| flee / flea |
1. My dog has a _____ on his tail.
2. Did the cats _____ when the dog barked?

| beats / beets |
3. Mother _____ the eggs with the mixer.
4. Those _____ are from the garden.

| right / write |
5. Please _____ me a letter soon.
6. I lost my _____ shoe!

| scent / cent |
7. I like the _____ of the spices.
8. I have one _____ in my pocket.

| won / one |
9. We _____ the game.
10. I have _____ dollar in the bank.

| dew / due |
11. The book is _____ on Friday.
12. The grass is wet from _____.

| no / know |
13. Do you _____ her name?
14. There is _____ more candy.

| creek / creak |
15. Frogs live in the _____.
16. Does that door _____ when opened?

Name _____ Skill: Homophones

Write the missing word in each sentence.

| way / weigh |
1. How much does the puppy _____?
2. Which _____ do you walk home?

| not / knot |
3. I am _____ going to be late.
4. Can you untie the _____?

| our / hour |
5. That is _____ house.
6. We will be home in an _____.

| eight / ate |
7. He _____ two hot dogs.
8. There are _____ people here.

| here / hear |
9. Did you _____ the news?
10. Put the letter in _____.

| too / two |
11. Can you come _____?
12. She has _____ sisters.

| bee / be |
13. I was stung by a _____.
14. Will you _____ home at three?

| pair / pear |
15. Pick a _____ from the tree.
16. I need a new _____ of shoes.

Name _____   Skill: Classifying

Title, Please

Find the title in the Title Box that best names each group of things listed below. Write the title on the line above each list.

Title Box

| Sounds | Colors | Vegetables | Cities |
| Insects | Shapes | Landforms | Feelings |

1. _____
   carrots, broccoli, peas, beans, asparagus

2. _____
   Boston, Dallas, Detroit, Miami, Denver

3. _____
   pop, bang, whoosh, crash, splat

4. _____
   circle, rectangle, triangle, square, oval

5. _____
   orchid, tan, maroon, turquoise, beige

6. _____
   lonely, excited, worried, surprised, scared

7. _____
   mountains, valleys, hills, plateaus, plains

8. _____
   fly, beetle, bee, hornet, ant, moth

Brainwork! Make a list of five words for each of these titles: Months, Flowers, and Famous People.

Name _____   Skill: Classifying

Word Exchange

Look at the words in the Word Box. Then look at each group of words below it. First cross out the word in the group that does not belong. Then write the word from the Word Box that does belong.

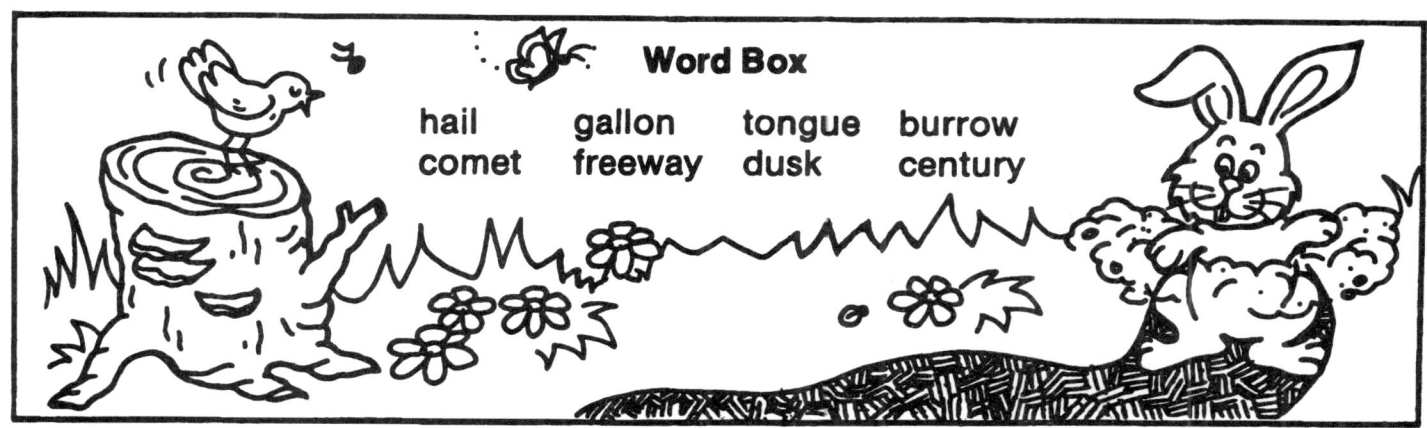

Word Box

hail gallon tongue burrow
comet freeway dusk century

1. sun planet stars moon violin meteor _____	2. eyes foot teeth nose ears cheeks _____
3. teaspoon liter quart cup pint several _____	4. nest barn library cave hive den _____
5. path highway trail street car road _____	6. lightning storm thunder mutter rain blizzard _____
7. sunrise dinner morning noonday afternoon evening _____	8. paddle decade month year day hour _____

Brainwork! Write a title for each list above.

Name _____ Skill: Analogies

How Are They Alike?

Read and think about each sentence. Fill in the ○ next to the word that correctly completes the sentence. Write the word on the line.

1. Cut is to scissors

   as slice is to _____.

   ○ bread
   ○ knife

2. Boat is to lake

   as ship is to _____.

   ○ ocean
   ○ sail

3. Eye is to see

   as ear is to _____.

   ○ hear
   ○ ring

4. Cup is to drink

   as plate is to _____.

   ○ wash
   ○ eat

5. Ink is to pen

   as paint is to _____.

   ○ picture
   ○ brush

6. Thermometer is to temperature

   as clock is to _____.

   ○ time
   ○ hour

7. Chick is to hen

   as kitten is to _____.

   ○ cat
   ○ cute

8. Toe is to foot

   as finger is to _____.

   ○ nail
   ○ hand

Brainwork! Write to tell how each of these pairs are alike: clothes and fur, hive and nest, syrup and jelly.

Name _____ Skill: Analogies

How Is It?

Read and think about each sentence. Choose the word from the Word Box that correctly completes the sentence. Write it on the line.

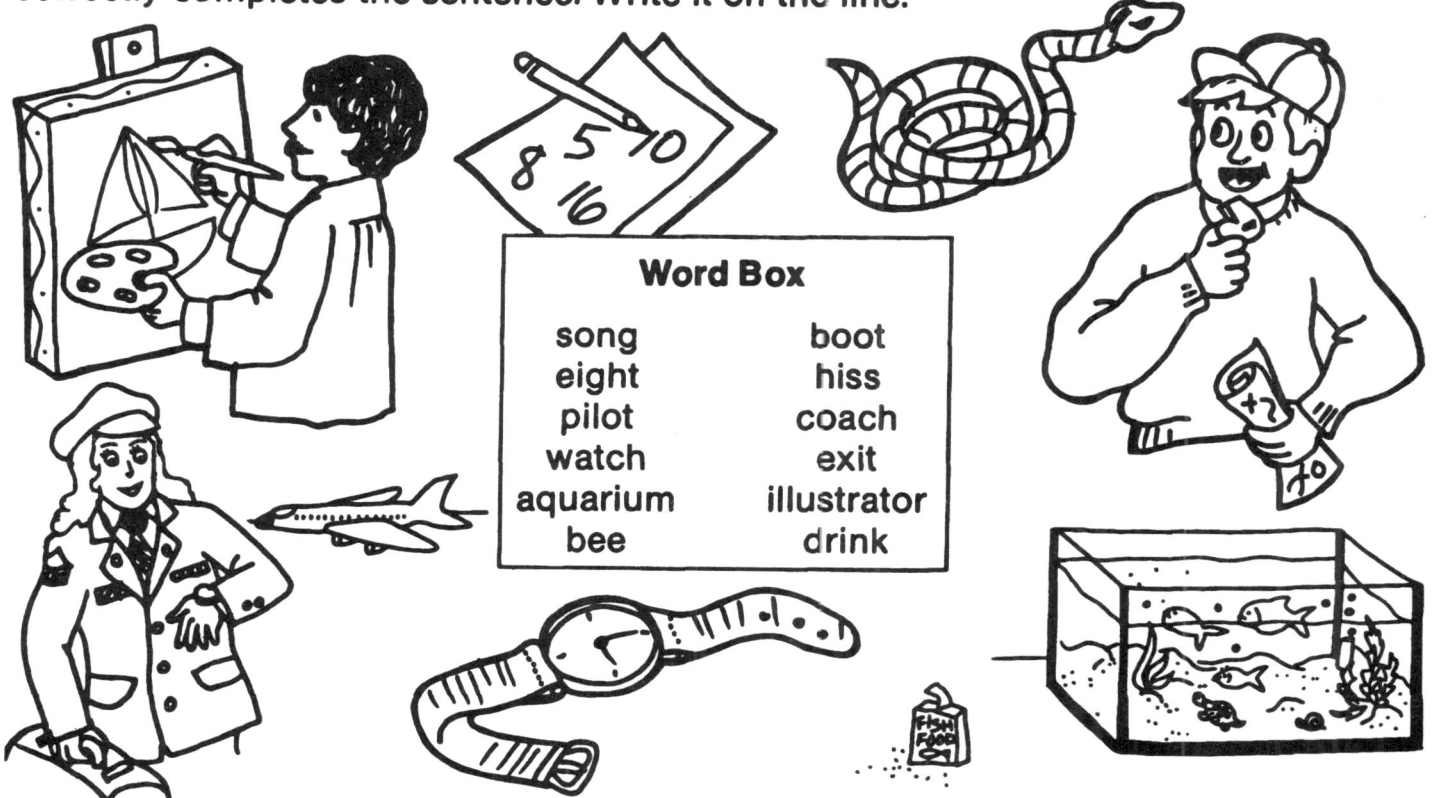

Word Box

song	boot
eight	hiss
pilot	coach
watch	exit
aquarium	illustrator
bee	drink

1. Teacher is to student as _____ is to player.
2. Five is to ten as _____ is to sixteen.
3. Writer is to book as _____ is to picture.
4. Ring is to finger as _____ is to arm.
5. Driver is to bus as _____ is to airplane.
6. Meow is to cat as _____ is to snake.
7. Out is to in as _____ is to enter.
8. Cage is to parakeet as _____ is to fish.
9. Eat is to hungry as _____ is to thirsty.
10. Story is to read as _____ is to sing.
11. Bear is to den as _____ is to hive.
12. Glove is to hand as _____ is to foot.

Brainwork! Choose one of the sentences above. Explain why it is true.

Name _____   Skill: Multiple meanings

What Do You Mean?

Look at the list below. Two different meanings are given for each word.

iris	1) a type of flower	2) colored part of the eye
perch	1) a type of fish	2) a bird's resting place
bill	1) notice of money owed	2) a bird's beak
trunk	1) storage area of a car	2) an elephant's nose
ruler	1) a person who governs	2) a tool for measuring
spring	1) to leap forward	2) a coil of wire
log	1) a daily record	2) section of a tree

Decide which meaning the boldfaced word has in each sentence below. Fill in ① or ②. Then write the meaning on the line.

① ② A. I had enough money to pay the **bill**.
_____

① ② B. We put the suitcases in the **trunk**.
_____

① ② C. You'll need a **ruler** to check the length.
_____

① ② D. Keep a **log** of your progress.
_____

① ② E. A purple **iris** is growing in the garden.
_____

① ② F. The clock needs a new **spring**.
_____

① ② G. Put another **log** on the fire.
_____

① ② H. I think I caught a **perch**.
_____

① ② I. She was the nation's **ruler**.
_____

① ② J. A duck has an orange **bill**.
_____

Brainwork! Use a dictionary. Write three different meanings for *dash*. Then write three sentences that use the word's different meanings.

Name _____ Skill: Vocabulary

That's Trite!

How many times have you described something as *nice* when you could have said *pleasant, friendly, pretty,* or *kind*? Words that are overused are said to be **trite**.

Look at each list of words. Choose the trite word from the Word Box that the list describes. Write it on the line.

Word Box
tell   dark   place   look   big   little

1. _____
huge, immense, gigantic, mammoth, colossal, enormous

2. _____
space, spot, area, region, location, site, position

3. _____
inform, notify, relate, explain, reveal, express

4. _____
gaze, glance, study, survey, behold, peek, stare, observe

5. _____
tiny, puny, petite, small, miniature

6. _____
shadowy, dim, unlit, gloomy, dusky, murky

Each sentence below contains two trite words from the Word Box. Write the sentence on the line replacing the trite words with more descriptive words from the lists above.

A. The whale seemed big next to the little fish.

_____

_____

B. The car ran out of gas in a dark place.

_____

C. Look at the sky and tell what you see.

_____

Brainwork! Write the three sentences again. This time use different words to replace the trite words.

Name _____   Skill: Commonly confused words

Clear Up the Confusion

Choose and write the correct word from each pair to complete the sentences.
If you are not sure, clear up the confusion with a dictionary.

series / serious
1. We had a _____ talk.
2. I've collected the whole _____ .

united / untied
3. My shoe always comes _____ .
4. We gave a _____ cheer for the team.

angel / angle
5. The ball bounced off at an _____ .
6. The _____ costume was white.

weather / whether
7. I don't know _____ to buy it or not.
8. I hope the _____ will be nice.

intend / attend
9. I _____ to finish it soon.
10. I cannot _____ your party.

lose / loose
11. The knob on the radio is _____ .
12. I hope you didn't _____ my phone number.

accept / except
13. I _____ your invitation to come.
14. Everyone was on time _____ me.

Brainwork! Is the head of your school a **principal** or a **principle**? Is Washington, D.C. the **capital** or the **capitol** of the U.S.? Clear up the confusion. Write definitions for each boldfaced word.

Name _____ Skill: Context

A Change of Heart

Each sentence below contains a "heart-y" word or phrase. Figure out its meaning and write it on the line. Choose from the meanings in the box.

"Heart-y" Meanings
- center
- saddened
- courage
- loved one
- friendly
- honest
- wanted
- from memory
- tender

1. We had a **heart-to-heart** talk. _____

2. I had **soft-hearted** feelings for the puppy. _____

3. It's in the **heart** of the city. _____

4. I was **heartbroken** by the news. _____

5. I didn't have the **heart** to tell her. _____

6. I know it **by heart**. _____

7. Grandma is a **sweetheart**. _____

8. He gave me a **hearty** welcome. _____

9. **I had my heart set on** the black kitten. _____

Brainwork! Explain the meaning of each of these expressions: *change of heart, won my heart, to my heart's content, take it to heart.*

Name _____ Skill: Context

What Do You Mean?

Choose a word from the Word Box to replace the boldfaced word in each sentence. Write it on the line. Use a dictionary to help you with new words.

Word Box
wrote	tray	real
trip	limp	wet
late	dry	force
winner	layer	reason

1. We took a **trek** up the mountainside.
   _____

2. The meat was served on a large **platter**.
   _____

3. The crown had **genuine** diamonds.
   _____

4. She missed the bus so she was **tardy**.
   _____

5. Without an umbrella I got **drenched**.
   _____

6. The desert soil was **parched**.
   _____

7. He **scrawled** a message on paper.
   _____

8. A **film** of ice covered the street.
   _____

9. The hurt player had to **hobble** off the field.
   _____

10. The **impact** of the wind broke off the branch.
    _____

11. The blue ribbon went to the **victor**.
    _____

12. What **motive** did you have for doing this?
    _____

Brainwork! Choose four of the sentences above to copy and illustrate.

Name _____   Skill: Getting meaning from context

Stay Tuned!

The name *television* comes from *tele-* meaning *far* in Greek, and *videre* meaning *to see* in Latin. Before 1950, the use of television was **rare**. Then, during a single **decade**, the ten-year period from 1950 to 1960, television became a part of almost every household in the United States. It **swiftly** became a **major** influence in people's lives. It changed the way they spent their time and let them see a whole new world right in their own homes.

Since the 1950s television has **evolved**, or grown and changed, to include uses in businesses, hospitals, schools, and law enforcement. As well as providing entertainment, television broadcasts business meetings and **monitors** hospital patients. It lets students study and observe world **events** as they happen, and even guards banks and prisons.

1. Which boldfaced word in the story means:

    a. a ten-year period? _____

    b. quickly? _____

    c. important? _____

    d. grown and changed? _____

    e. watches over? _____

    f. happenings? _____

    g. uncommon? _____

2. Where did the name for television come from?

    _____

    _____

    _____

3. How did television influence people's lives after 1950?

    _____

    _____

4. What do you think is television's most important use and why?

    _____

    _____

Brainwork! Tell about one important world event that millions of people witnessed on television.

Name _____ Skill: Scientific vocabulary

Volcanoes!

Volcanoes are special kinds of mountains. Under volcanoes, deep in the earth, is a layer of hot, liquid rock called **magma**. Volcanoes are formed when the magma is suddenly forced up through a crack in the **crust**, or surface, of the earth. This action, called **eruption**, spills the hot magma, or lava, out onto the crust. As it cools, it hardens and forms mounds.

Scientists classify volcanoes in three groups. The first group includes volcanoes that have not erupted in hundreds of years. These volcanoes are **extinct** and are unlikely to erupt again. The second group also includes volcanoes that have not erupted in many years but these volcanoes are thought to be capable of erupting again. These volcanoes are called **dormant**. The final group includes volcanoes that erupted not long ago and could erupt again at any time. These volcanoes are said to be **active**.

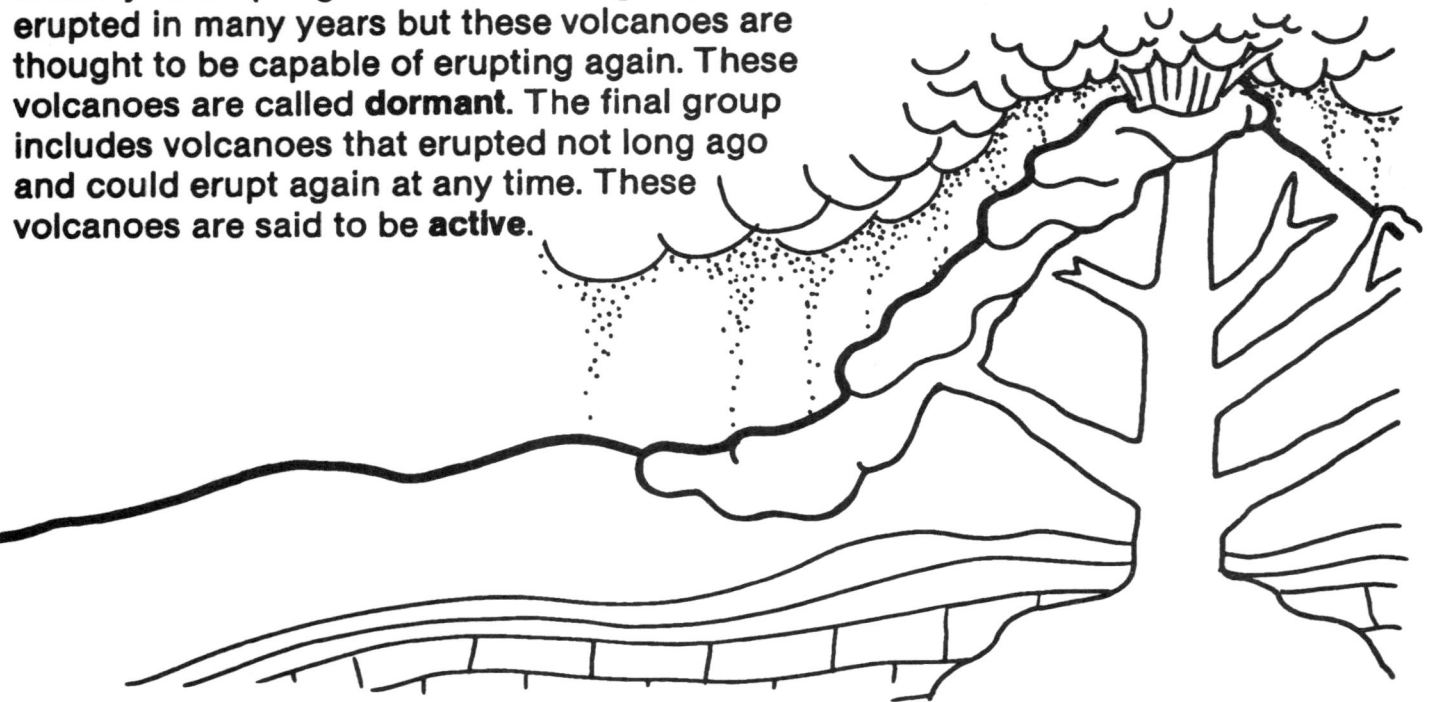

Find and write a boldfaced word from the story for each description.

1. _____ liquid rock beneath the earth
2. _____ group of volcanoes unlikely to erupt
3. _____ the outer surface of the earth
4. _____ action that forces magma through the crust
5. _____ group of volcanoes that have recently erupted
6. _____ group of volcanoes that have not erupted in many years but still may erupt

Brainwork! Mount St. Helens in the state of Washington erupted on May 18, 1980. Find out about that event. Write your findings.

Name _____ Skill: Technical vocabulary

Computer Data

Computers may seem "smart" but they cannot think. The only thing they can do is follow a set of instructions called a **program** which must be written by a person. The computer **hardware** (machinery) and **software** (programs) work together.

For the computer to work, a person must enter **data**, or information, into the computer. This is called **input**. New data is entered by typing on a **keyboard** that has letters and symbols like a typewriter. Data may be stored on a **disk** which is used to record and save information.

Next, the computer "reads" the data and follows the instructions of the program. The program may tell it to organize the data, compare it to other data, or store it for later use. This is called data **processing**.

When the processing is complete, the computer can display the **results** either on the screen or printed on paper as a **printout**.

Find and write a boldfaced word from the story for each description.

1. _____ used to save and record information
2. _____ organizing, comparing, or storing data
3. _____ results printed on paper
4. _____ set of instructions for a computer
5. _____ computer machinery
6. _____ entering data
7. _____ computer programs
8. _____ where data is entered

Label each picture below **hardware** or **software**.

9. _____   10. _____

Brainwork! Explain why some people think computers seem "smart."

Name _____   Skill: Latin prefixes

Words From Latin

Some English words are made with prefixes borrowed from Latin.

Use the meanings of the Latin prefixes in the Word Box to help you write the English word for each definition below.

Word Box

com- = together	**semi-** = half; partly	**dis-** = opposite
pre- = before	**re-** = back; again	**sub-** = below

1. a half circle _____semicircle_____
2. below freezing _____
3. heat again _____
4. view before _____
5. opposite of agree _____
6. write again _____
7. gain back _____
8. below soil _____
9. partial darkness _____
10. press together _____
11. opposite of honest _____
12. appear again _____
13. opposite of respect _____
14. partly automatic _____

Brainwork! English borrows parts of words from Greek, too. The prefix *tele-* means *far*. Write five words you know that begin with *tele-*. Then write their meanings.

Name _____

Directions:
- Circle the words that tell (who).
- Draw one line under words that tell where.
- Make a box around words that name [things].

library	apple	baby	factory
mailman	church	flashlight	librarian
kitchen	car	school	key
pencil	doctor	toothbrush	garage
teacher	store	hospital	grandfather

Directions:
- Put a △ on things found in a kitchen.
- Draw two lines under things found in a garage.
- Make a dotted circle around things found in a (bedroom).

car	paintbrushes	stove	can opener
spoons	hammer	sheets	toolbox
pillow	dresser	clothing	saucer
sink	alarm clock	drill	bed
bicycles	frying pan	blanket	refrigerator

Directions: In each box above put a ★ in front of the word that would appear first in the dictionary. Make a **X** in front of the word in each box that would appear last in the dictionary.

Name _____

```
NW            N            NE




W                          E




SW            S            SE
```

Directions:
- ☐ Draw a line to connect **N** to **S** and **E** to **W**.
- ☐ Draw a line to connect **NE** to **SW** and **SE** to **NW**.
- ☐ Print your initials in the section between **N** and **NE**.
- ☐ Write your age in the section between **SW** and **W**.
- ☐ Print a friend's first name in capital letters between **S** and **SE**.
- ☐ Write the month and date you were born in **SW** to **S**.
- ☐ In **E** to **SE** write the name of your favorite book or TV show.
- ☐ In **NE** to **E** draw a picture of your favorite food and print it's name.
- ☐ Between **NW** and **N** draw a picture of your favorite sport.
- ☐ In **W** to **NW** write what you want to be when you grow up.

Name _____

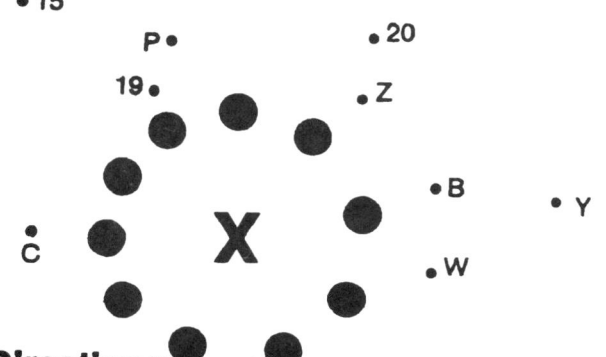

Directions:
☐ Make a circle around each **X**. Darken the ⊗ with your pencil.
☐ Connect the large dots around each ⊗ to make a larger circle.
  Make a line to connect:
  ☐ W to E to 4 to 16 to 18 to F.
  ☐ A to 9 to 5 to 6 to A.
  ☐ M to H.
  ☐ 12 to 17 to D to 11.
  ☐ 12 to 13 to K to 2.
  ☐ W to B to Z to 19 to C.
  ☐ C to 15 to 2.
  ☐ P to 21 to 8 to 10 to 7 to Y to 20 to P.
  ☐ 1 to 21.
  ☐ 13 to G.
☐ Make a wavy line from 11 to Q to R to F.
☐ Make a small circle around 13. Darken the circle.

© Frank Schaffer Publications, Inc.   FS-32032 Reading Activities

Name _____

Directions:
☐ Learn how to write checks by looking at sample check 301.
☐ Write check 302 to Super Shirts for $4.00 to pay for a T-shirt on July 20, 1996.
☐ Pay Nancy Gomez with check 303 for the newspaper on August 1, 1996. The cost of the newspaper delivery is $3.75.

301
_____ July 3 _____ 19 96
Pay to the Order of _Soccer Shop_____ $ 12.50
_Twelve and 50/100_____ Dollars
VILLAGE BANK
For _cleats_____   _Don Gruber_____

302
_____ 19 ____
Pay to the Order of _____ $ _____
_____ Dollars
VILLAGE BANK
For _____   _____

303
_____ 19 ____
Pay to the Order of _____ $ _____
_____ Dollars
VILLAGE BANK
For _____   _____

Name _____

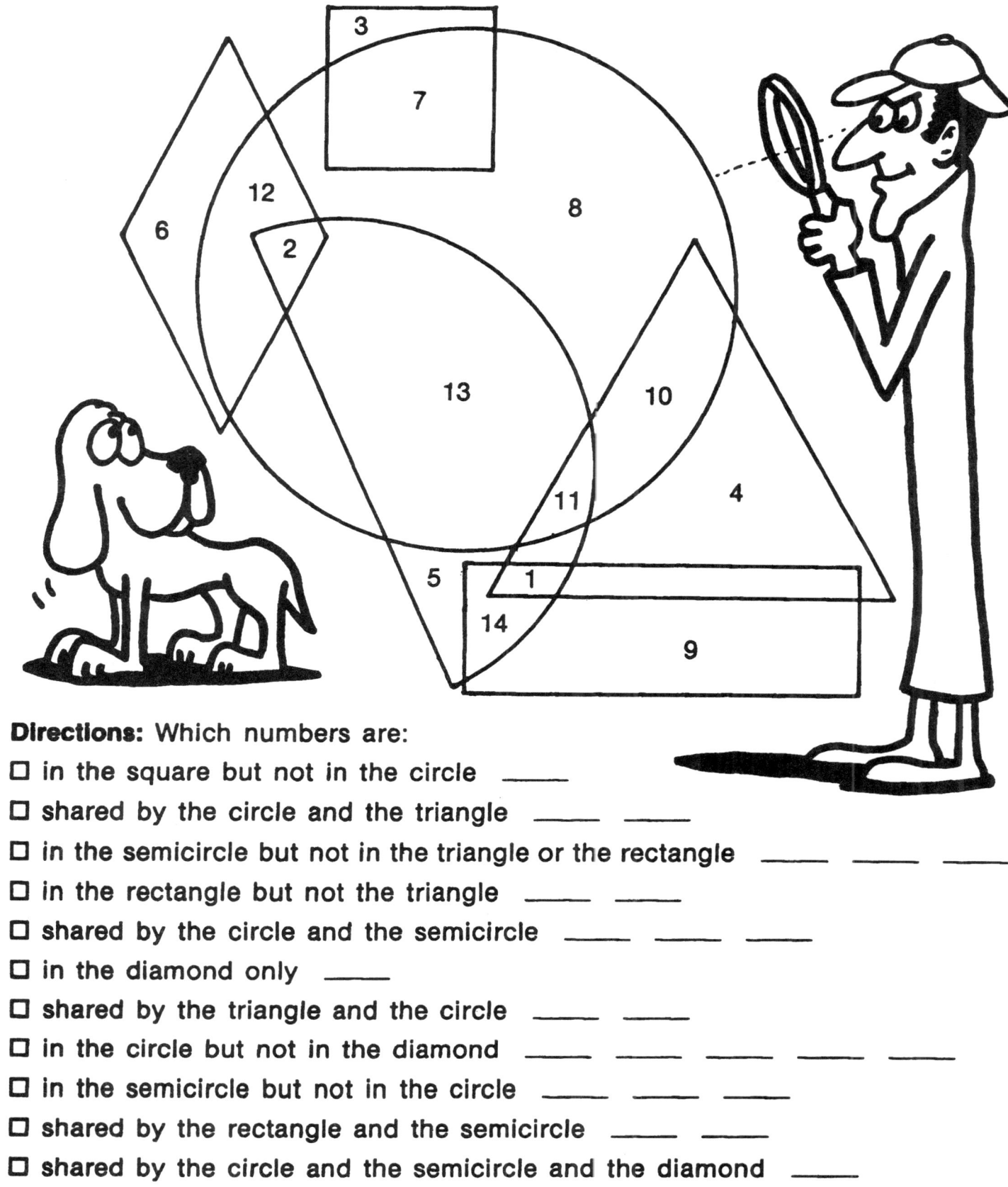

Directions: Which numbers are:
- ☐ in the square but not in the circle ___
- ☐ shared by the circle and the triangle ___ ___
- ☐ in the semicircle but not in the triangle or the rectangle ___ ___ ___
- ☐ in the rectangle but not the triangle ___ ___
- ☐ shared by the circle and the semicircle ___ ___ ___
- ☐ in the diamond only ___
- ☐ shared by the triangle and the circle ___ ___
- ☐ in the circle but not in the diamond ___ ___ ___ ___
- ☐ in the semicircle but not in the circle ___ ___ ___
- ☐ shared by the rectangle and the semicircle ___ ___
- ☐ shared by the circle and the semicircle and the diamond ___

Name _____

Directions: Follow the directions after each sentence.

1. Nan and her sister built a two-story treehouse in the huge oak tree.
   - ☐ Circle the shortest word in the above sentence.
   - ☐ Underline two words that describe the tree.
   - ☐ Make a dotted line under the girl's name.

2. We hiked and fished on our camping trip in _____.
   - ☐ Write the name of a summer month on the ____.
   - ☐ Put an **X** on the word that tells the kind of trip.
   - ☐ Underline two activities done on the trip.

3. _____ scored two goals in the soccer game yesterday morning.
   - ☐ Write your name on the ____.
   - ☐ Put a box around the number word.
   - ☐ There are two words that tell when. Circle them both.

4. My grandmother is flying out to visit from _____.
   - ☐ Write the name of a city on the ____.
   - ☐ Make a dotted line under the person word.
   - ☐ How is grandmother making the trip? Underline one word that tells how.

5. Don used _____ pieces of wood to make the birdhouse for the robins.
   - ☐ Write a number word between four and nine on the ____.
   - ☐ Circle the word that tells who will live in the house.
   - ☐ Who made the birdhouse? Draw a dotted line under the name.

6. I had to pay _____ cents because my library book was late.
   - ☐ Write a number word between eleven and seventeen on the ____.
   - ☐ Circle one word that tells why I had to pay.
   - ☐ Put an **X** on the word that names a place.

7. After dinner I must do my homework or practice the piano.
   - ☐ Underline the shortest word in the sentence.
   - ☐ Draw a box around the word that names an instrument.
   - ☐ Circle the word that begins with the first letter of the alphabet.

8. My older brother works in a television store in the shopping center.
   - ☐ Who works in the store? Underline two words about the person.
   - ☐ Draw two lines under the one word that tells the kind of store.
   - ☐ Where is the store? Circle two words.

9. Mother's plane arrived late because of the snowstorm in the mountains.
   - ☐ Draw a dotted line under one word that describes a kind of weather.
   - ☐ Circle the word that tells where.
   - ☐ Put an **X** on the person word.

10. My baby sister takes one nap from two to four o'clock in the afternoon.
    - ☐ Who takes a nap? Put one box around two words that tell.
    - ☐ How many naps each day? Underline one word that tells.
    - ☐ Draw two dotted lines under one word that tells when she naps.

Name _____

Directions: Follow the directions after each sentence.

1. Dad built a huge wood hutch for our pet rabbits.
   ☐ Circle the word that tells who built the hutch.
   ☐ Make a dot over each vowel in the sentence.
   ☐ Make a dotted line under the two words that describe the hutch.

2. My older brother's team won the basketball game last night.
   ☐ Put a small triangle over the word that names a sport.
   ☐ Draw two lines under the word that means "a group of people".
   ☐ Circle the word that tells a time of day.

3. My dog Toto will sit, roll over and bark if you give him a treat.
   ☐ Put a box around the dog's name.
   ☐ Draw two lines under the three tricks the dog will do.
   ☐ Circle the words in the sentence that have three letters.

4. I mailed the letter in the mailbox at the corner of First and Maple Streets.
   ☐ Draw a dotted line under the words in the sentence that have two letters.
   ☐ Circle the two street names.
   ☐ Write an **X** on the word that tells what you did with the letter.

5. Jake and I are building a fort under the tree in his back yard.
   ☐ Make a box around the word that tells what they are building.
   ☐ Three living things are named in the sentence - circle them.
   ☐ Make a dotted line under the word that is the opposite of front.

6. Mary and _____ caught three fish over by the big rock.
   ☐ Write your name on the _____ .
   ☐ Circle the number word.
   ☐ Make two dotted lines under one word that means the same as "large".

7. Mother jogs three miles every morning before breakfast.
   ☐ Make a box around the word that tells how mother travels the three miles.
   ☐ Make a small triangle over the number word.
   ☐ Circle the word that names a meal.

8. I found our neighbor's dog on the way home from school.
   ☐ Two words in the sentence name a place - underline them both.
   ☐ Make a dot under every vowel (a e i o u) in the sentence.
   ☐ Make a box around the word that tells who found the dog.

9. My brother has four sports posters on the wall in his bedroom.
   ☐ Make two lines under one word that tells how many posters.
   ☐ Circle words that end with "s".
   ☐ Make a triangle above the word that tells who owns the posters.

10. I am allowed to watch television for one hour each day.
    ☐ Draw a dotted line under the word that means the opposite of night.
    ☐ Write an **X** on the number word.
    ☐ Draw two lines under the word that means the same as "see".

Name _____

Directions:

☐ Read the directions in the column on the left. Look at the column on the right.
☐ If they've been done correctly, put a star ★ in the box.
☐ If they've been done wrong, make them right. The first one is a sample.

1.	Print the first three days of the week in abc order.	★ Monday Sunday Tuesday
2.	Put a dot over the vowels (a e i o u) in each word.	ráin kíte hút sámé enóúgh rúnning
3.	Make a box around words with one syllable.	hat apple friend surprise fun I
4.	Draw two lines under words that name places.	book library teacher bus home school
5.	Put an X on words that do not rhyme with date.	crate mXde afrXid mate late
6.	Make one line under things found on farms. Make two lines under things found in cities.	hay bus barn cow escalator farmer
7.	Put two dots over things that are alive.	trëe puppy truck bäby book
8.	Circle objects that work by electricity.	(television) magazine pen (radio) (light)
9.	Cross out the word that does not belong.	hand foot arm head shoe knee
10.	Draw a dotted line under the heaviest thing.	elephant pencil apple dime paper
11.	Put a triangle over things people can do.	sing△ dance△ cry△ laugh△ fly△
12.	Capitalize the names of the months.	may spring July June summer April August fall
13.	Underline words that have a beginning consonant blend.	chart lunch drop break stop
14.	Make a / to divide compound words.	base/ball fire/house can't don't tooth/brush I'm

Name _____

Directions: Follow the directions below each grid. Count across, then up and make a dot for each pair of numbers. Connect the dots in the order you made them on the grid.

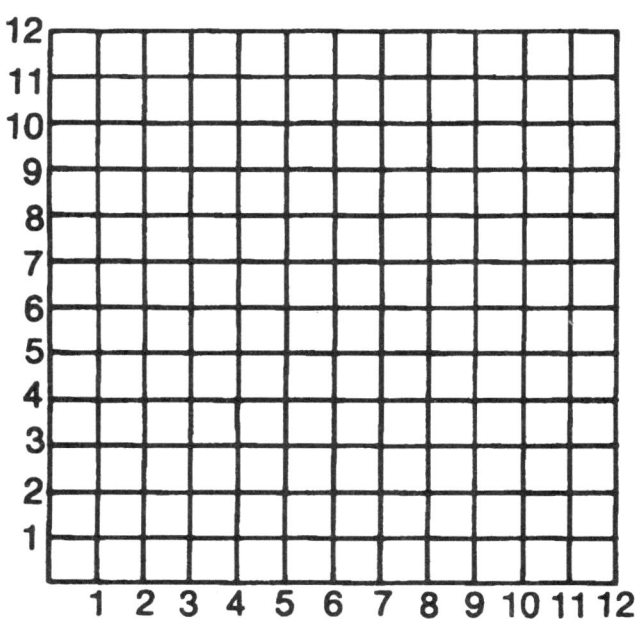
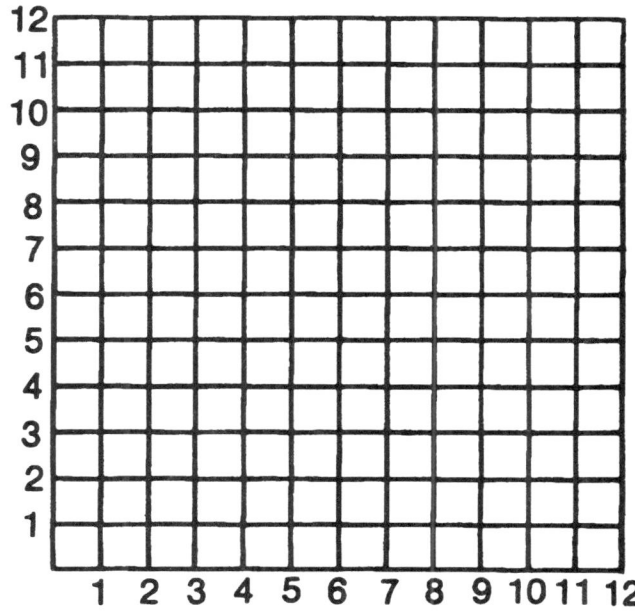

1. 7,8	10. 5,9	1. 7,3	13. 9,10
2. 9,9	11. 7,8	2. 9,5	14. 8,10
3. 10,8	12. 7,10	3. 9,4	15. 8,11
4. 11,7	13. 8,11	4. 7,3	16. 7,12
5. 11,5	14. 10,12	5. 5,5	17. 6,11
6. 8,2	15. 11,12	6. 5,4	18. 6,10
7. 5,2	16. 9,10	7. 7,3	19. 5,10
8. 3,4	17. 7,10	8. 7,8	20. 5,11
9. 3,7	18. 7,12	9. 8,8	21. 4,12
		10. 10,10	22. 4,10
		11. 10,12	23. 6,8
		12. 9,11	24. 7,8

Name _____

Directions: Magic Math Squares add up to the same number when you add across or down the rows.
☐ Find the solution for each math problem and write it in the answer column.
☐ Write the answers in the Magic ×÷ Square.

Box	Problem	Answer
☐ Q	36 ÷ 6	6
☐ P	21 ÷ 7	___
☐ B	18 ÷ 9	___
☐ X	32 ÷ 4	___
☐ D	8 × 0	___
☐ N	16 ÷ 2	___
☐ R	6 × 0	___
☐ T	24 ÷ 6	___
☐ S	16 ÷ 4	___
☐ C	3 × 6	___
☐ W	20 ÷ 10	___
☐ O	3 × 7	___
☐ A	30 ÷ 5	___
☐ Y	27 ÷ 9	___
☐ Z	2 × 8 + 1	___
☐ M	2 × 9	___

Magic ×÷ Square

A	Q	M	R
	6		
D	T	N	C
O	P	B	S
Y	Z	W	X

☐ Find out the number by adding down or across. The number is ___ .

Write addition or subtraction problems for the Magic +– Square.

Box	Problem
☐ O	7 + 5
☐ U	___
☐ S	___
☐ R	___
☐ P	___
☐ Q	___
☐ M	___
☐ T	___
☐ N	___

Magic +– Square

O	T	Q
12	2	10
M	U	N
8	11	5
R	P	S
4	11	9

☐ Find out the number. The number is ___ .

Name _____

Directions: At the bottom of the page:
- ☐ On line 18 write the letter below the Ukulele.
- ☐ On line 4 write the letter above the Violin.
- ☐ Write the letter on the Classical Guitar on line 3.
- ☐ Write the letter below the Violin on line 1.
- ☐ Write the letter between the Cello and Mandolin on line 9.
- ☐ On line 8 write the letter above the Banjo.
- ☐ On line 15 write the letter between the Violin and Ukulele.
- ☐ Write the letter on the Cello on line 16.
- ☐ On line 10 write the letter below the Banjo.
- ☐ Write the letter above the Ukulele on line 14.
- ☐ On line 19 write the letter on the Banjo.
- ☐ On line 2 write the letter between the Banjo and Classical Guitar.
- ☐ Write the letter above the Cello on line 6.
- ☐ Write the letter on the Violin on line 13.
- ☐ On line 12 write the letter between the Mandolin and Classical Guitar.
- ☐ Write the letter between the Violin and Banjo on line 17.
- ☐ On line 5 write the letter above the Mandolin.
- ☐ Write the letter below the Cello on line 11.
- ☐ On line 7 write the letter below the Mandolin.

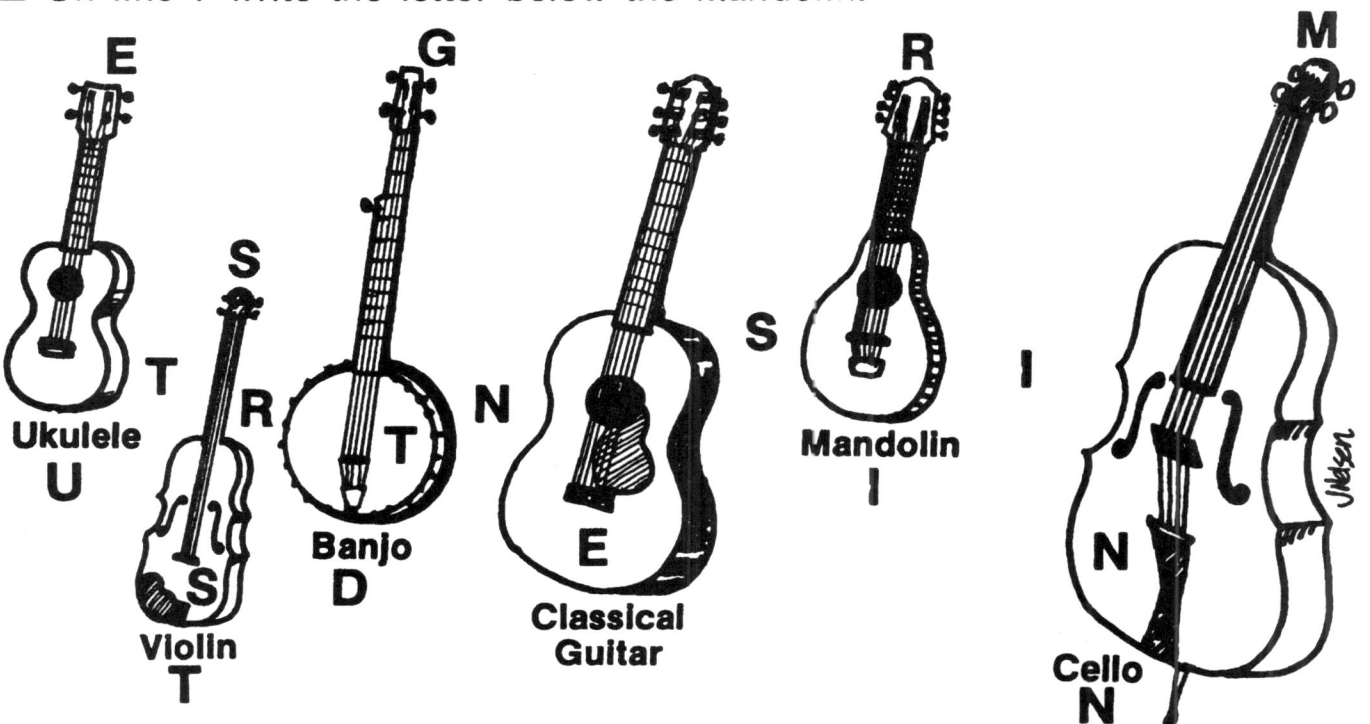

___ ___ ___ ___ ___ ___ ___ ___ ___ ___ ___ ___ ___ ___ ___ ___ ___ ___ ___
13   1   17   7   16   8   14 10   9   2   12   15   5   18   6   3   11   19   4

71

Name _____

Directions: Read the clues and write a word from the list. Then write the letters on the correct line in the Mystery Saying Box. The mystery saying was made up by Benjamin Franklin.

Clues

☐ a kind of plant ___ ___ ___ ___ ___
            43 17 14 41 15

☐ opposite of night ___ ___ ___
             47   2 44

☐ 365 days ___ ___ ___ ___
          5 25 27 18

☐ opposite of love ___ ___ ___ ___
             31 23 42   9

☐ group of people ___ ___ ___ ___
            16 39 12 22

☐ kind of flower ___ ___ ___ ___
            3   7 26 51

☐ opposite of us ___ ___ ___ ___
           35 36 21 28

☐ opposite of lower ___ ___ ___ ___ ___
              13 45 49 20 32

☐ a rule ___ ___ ___
        4 40 48

☐ opposite of good ___ ___ ___
             8 29 10

☐ very small ___ ___ ___ ___
           6 19 46 37

☐ opposite of sleep ___ ___ ___ ___
              38 33 24 11

☐ part of a camera ___ ___ ___ ___
             34   1 30 50

Word List

holly	rose	year	hate
them	lens	law	tiny
raise	wake	team	bad
day			

Mystery Saying Box

___ ___ ___ ___ ___ ___ ___ ___ ___ ___ .
 1   2   3   4   5   6   7   8   9 10

___ ___ ___ ___ ___ ___ ___ ___ ___ ___ ___ .
11 12 13 14 15   16 17   18 19 20 21

___ ___ ___ ___ ___ ___ ___ ___ ___ ___ ___ ___ ___ ___ ,
22 23 24 25 26   27   28 29   30 31 32 33 34 35 36 37

___ ___ ___ ___ ___ ___ ___ ___ ___ ___ ___ ___ ___ .
38 39 40 41 42 43   44 45 46   47 48 49 50 51

Name _____

Directions: Follow the directions to figure out how fast some animals can travel. Write your answer on the _____ .

On Land	Miles Per Hour	
Snake	2	
Man	____	(ten times faster than snake)
Elephant	____	(five mph faster than man)
Cheetah	____	(two times as fast as elephant, plus man's speed)
Ostrich	____	(twice as fast as man)
Jack Rabbit	____	(five mph faster than ostrich)
Greyhound	____	(same speed as ostrich)

In the Air		
Housefly	5	
Bat	____	(three times as fast as housefly)
Bluejay	____	(five mph faster than housefly)
Dragonfly	____	(ten times faster than housefly)
Hummingbird	____	(ten mph faster than the dragonfly)
Owl	____	(subtract speed of bluejay from hummingbird)

In the Water		
Goldfish	4	
Man	____	(one mph faster than goldfish)
Barracuda	____	(six times faster than man)
Sea Turtle	____	(ten mph slower than barracuda)
Whale	____	(four times faster than man)
Dolphin	____	(add speeds of man and sea turtle)

☐ Circle the fastest animal in each category.
☐ Make a box around the slowest animal in each category.

Name _____

Directions: Read each statement. Decide if it is true or false. Circle the answer. Write the letter under true or false in the correct box at the bottom of the page.

	True	False
1. All birds can fly.	T	(Q)
2. Sometimes it rains at night.	U	R
3. Three is not a number between two and four.	F	B
4. Boys are always bigger than girls.	Q	C
5. Girls can play football.	N	A
6. Everyone likes ice cream.	L	A
7. Some trees lose leaves in winter.	E	U
8. All fish do not live in the ocean.	A	I
9. You should brush your teeth after eating.	R	E
10. All corners have traffic lights.	U	Y
11. Bridges are never made of wood.	I	T
12. Some plants have flowers.	F	T
13. Kittens grow up to be cats.	N	E
14. Tigers never live in zoos.	R	E
15. You can always see a rainbow when it stops raining.	C	T
16. Boats never sink.	E	C
17. All men work in offices.	K	A
18. Pencils are not always sharp.	O	D
19. Most dogs like bones.	I	B
20. Tables are not always made of wood.	U	S
21. Ice is cold.	T	L
22. Spoons can only be made from metal.	S	O
23. Books can have fewer than ten pages.	A	S
24. February is between January and March.	R	N
25. You must be ten years old to go to school.	N	N
26. Not all shoes have laces.	K	D
27. All people can read.	E	S
28. Ballet dancers are never men.	N	T
29. Tea is not always hot.	E	C
30. Some people like popcorn.	I	Y
31. Tiny babies cannot count to ten.	S	S
32. Light bulbs always light.	A	S

16	24	2	7		23	13	27		12	6	22	32	15		1	20	14	28	11	30	18	5	31
															Q								

17	8	25		3	29		21	9	19	4	26	10
												!

Name _____

Directions: Read the list of clues below to find the most unusual animal on the animal list. Circle the animals as you read the clues. When you have followed the directions you will have one animal not circled. Check off the boxes as you answer each clue.

Circle the animals that:
- ☐ have three letters
- ☐ have twelve letters
- ☐ end in F
- ☐ end in two consonants
- ☐ have a Z
- ☐ have more vowels than consonants
- ☐ have C as the first letter
- ☐ have two L's
- ☐ have five letters
- ☐ have an I
- ☐ have a vowel as the second letter

☐ You should have the name of one animal left. Draw a box around that animal.

☐ Look in the encyclopedia to find out why that animal is unusual. Put your answer here.

_____
_____
_____
_____

Animal List
wolf
dingo
platypus
gibbon
giraffe
chinchilla
yak
gorilla
cheetah
zebra
ostrich
aardvark
elephant
kangaroo
deer
moose
tarantula
caribou
walrus
hippopotamus
snake

Name _____

Directions: Read the list of clues below about the first team that won the SUPER BOWL four times. Circle the teams as you read the clues. When you have followed all directions you will have one team that is not circled. That will be the team.

Circle the teams that:
- ☐ have five letters
- ☐ have a K in them
- ☐ begin with a vowel
- ☐ have more than eleven letters
- ☐ end in I
- ☐ have a consonant as the second letter
- ☐ have X, Y or Z
- ☐ have A's
- ☐ have O's
- ☐ have E's
- ☐ You should have the name of one team left. Draw a box around the first team that won the SUPER BOWL four times.

NATIONAL FOOTBALL LEGUE

ATLANTA
BUFFALO
CHICAGO
CINCINNATI
CLEVELAND
DALLAS
DENVER
DETROIT
GREEN BAY
HOUSTON
INDIANAPOLIS
KANSAS CITY
LOS ANGELES RAIDERS
LOS ANGELES RAMS
MIAMI
MINNESOTA
NEW ENGLAND
NEW ORLEANS
NEW YORK GIANTS
NEW YORK JETS
PHILADELPHIA
PHOENIX
PITTSBURGH
SAN DIEGO
SAN FRANCISCO
SEATTLE
TAMPA
WASHINGTON

Name _____

Directions: Do the Birthday Math Puzzle.

☐ Write the number for the month you were born on the dotted line below.

Month you were born _ _ _ _

☐ multiply by 5   _____
☐ add 6   _____
☐ multiply by 4   _____
☐ add 9   _____
☐ multiply by 5   _____
☐ add the date you
  were born   _____
                       Total _____

☐ subtract 165 from total __ __ __ __

Jan.	1
Feb.	2
Mar.	3
Apr.	4
May	5
June	6
July	7
Aug.	8
Sept.	9
Oct.	10
Nov.	11
Dec.	12

the last two numbers tell the date you were born

the first number or numbers will will be the month you were born

"June first.."

Try the Birthday Math Puzzle with a friend's birthdate!

Name _____

Directions: Look at the floor plan of the bedroom. Draw a line to match each object with its location.

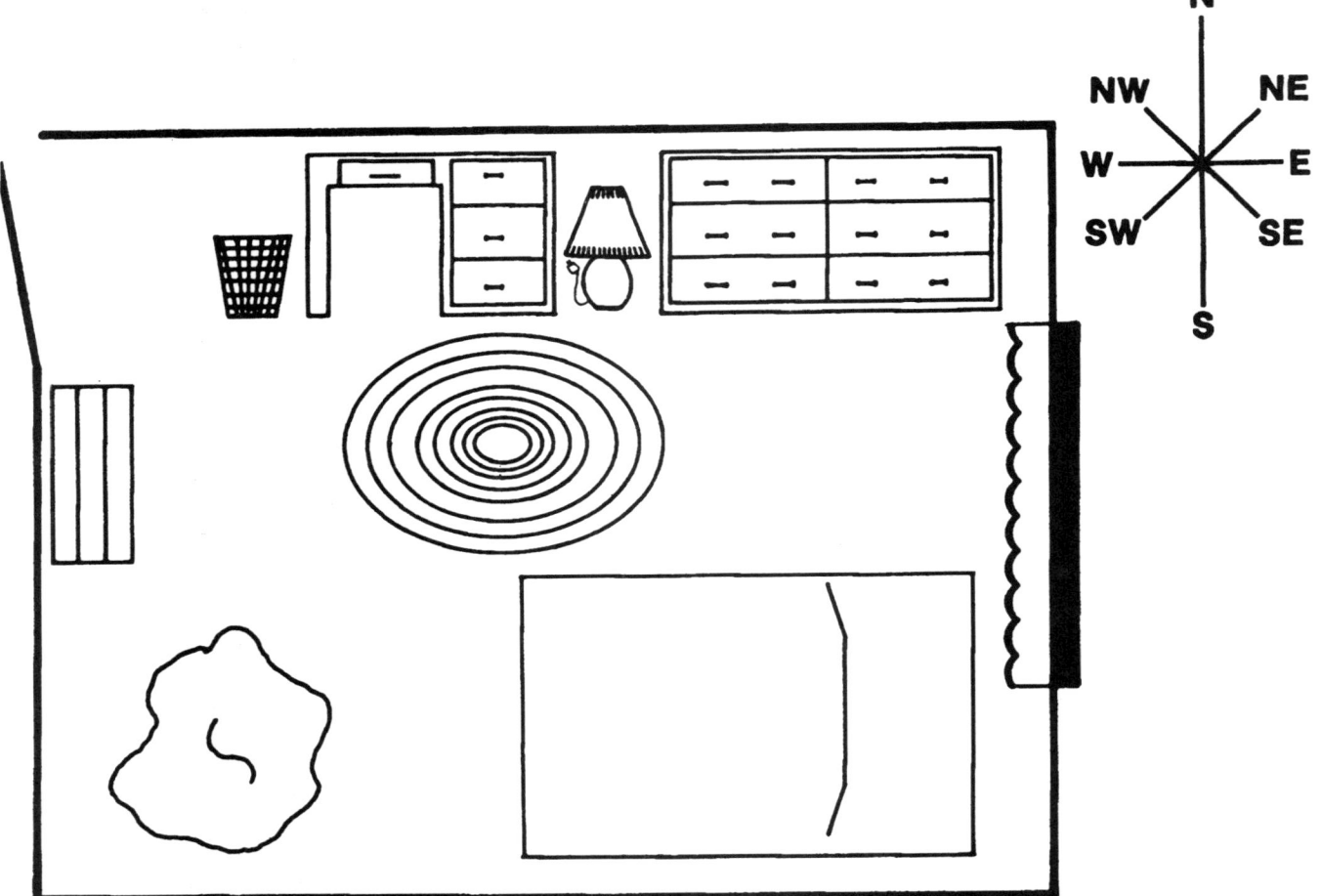

Objects	Location
window	north wall in east corner
doorway	center of east wall
beanbag chair	south wall in SE corner
wastebasket	north wall between lamp and wastebasket
bed	SW corner
desk	NW corner
lamp	center of room
rug	center of west wall
dresser	west side of desk
shelves	north wall between desk and dresser

Name _____

Directions: Add furniture to the floor plan of the house.

Back yard (south side of house)
- Diving Board - east end of pool 🗆
- Round Table and Three Chairs - in SW corner Ⓣ

Kitchen (south of garage)
- Square Table and Four Chairs - west wall Ⓣ
- Refrigerator - SE corner [R]
- Stove - west side of refrigerator
- Sink and Counter - NE corner

Living Room (south of kitchen)
- Small Round Table - NW corner Ⓣ
- Couch - west wall
- Two Chairs and a Small Square Table - south wall (Ⓣ)

#2 Bedroom (NE corner of house)
- Bed - east wall
- Dresser - west wall
- Chair - NW corner

#1 Bedroom (west of #2 bedroom)
- Bed - north wall
- Dresser - west wall
- Chair - SE corner

#3 Bedroom (south of hall)
- Bed - west wall
- Two Dressers - south wall
- Chair - NE corner
- Table - east wall beside chair Ⓣ

Name _____

About Your Heart

What is as big as a fist, has four rooms and works every second of your life? It's your heart! This amazing part of your body pumps blood. The blood delivers air and food to all the other parts of your body. Then the blood carries waste away and returns to your heart to begin again. Every time your heart beats, blood is sent through the body. A grown person's heart beats 72 times each minute. A newborn baby's heart beats 140 times each minute. Listen to your friend's heart through a cardboard tube.

1. **In the story, the word heart means:**
   a. a part of your body that is very important
   b. a part of your body that is not important
   c. a part of an automobile

2. **Another word for amazing is:**
   a. silly
   b. wonderful
   c. alike

3. **The opposite of works is:**
   a. studies
   b. allows
   c. plays

4. **A word in the story that sounds like cent is:**
   _____

5. **The word your stands for:**
   a. the person reading this
   b. a baby
   c. a grown person

6. **A word in the story that goes with fingers and hands is:**
   a. heart
   b. fist
   c. minute

★ On the back of this paper draw a picture of your heart. Write two sentences about why it is important.

Name _____

Indian Carvings

Have you ever seen **totem** poles? They are carved wooden poles. Totems were made by Indians who lived in Alaska, Washington, Oregon and northern California. Each pole was made from a tall tree whose branches were cut off. Then, they were smoothed with sharp iron tools called "toes". The poles were hollowed out on one side. The other side was carved into shapes of animals and people. Each pole tells a different story that the Indians want to remember.

1. **In the story, the words totem pole mean:**
   a. a drink made by Indians
   b. story-carvings on poles
   c. an Indian dance

2. **Another word for story is:**
   a. village
   b. place
   c. tale

3. **The opposite of off is:**
   a. in
   b. on
   c. under

4. **A word in the story that sounds like too is:**

5. **The word they stands for:**
   a. totem poles
   b. Indians
   c. pictures

6. **A word in the story that goes with cut and sawed is:**
   a. animals
   b. Indians
   c. chopped

★ **On the back of this paper draw a picture of a totem pole. Write a story about your totem.**

Name _____

Animal with a Pocket

Kangaroos live in **Australia**. <u>They</u> are **marsupials**. That means they carry their young in a special pocket. When the new joey is born, the mother licks its fur. Then he can climb easily to the safety of the pocket. When he is thirsty, he drinks his mother's milk. When his mother grazes, he can graze without leaving the pocket. He stays inside until he is strong enough to be on his own. Even then, if danger is near, he can dive back in—head first!

1. **In the story, the word <u>marsupial</u> means:**
   a. an animal who lays eggs
   b. an animal who has a special pocket for her baby
   c. animals who swim

2. **Another word for <u>stays</u> is:**
   a. remains
   b. leaves
   c. follows

3. **The opposite of <u>strong</u> is:**
   a. heavy
   b. good
   c. weak

4. **A word in the story that sounds like <u>fir</u> is:**
   _____

5. **The word <u>they</u> stands for:**
   a. feet
   b. kangaroos
   c. tail

6. **A word in the story that goes with <u>envelope</u> and <u>case</u> is:**
   a. pocket
   b. near
   c. dive

★ **On the back of this paper write a story about how different animals protect their babies.**

Great Games

Every four years, strong men and women race for gold and silver medals. This happens at the modern **Olympics** which began in 1896 in **Athens**, **Greece**. They were held there first to honor the ancient Greek Olympic events. There are summer and winter games. They are played in different cities in the world and include all kinds of sports. At one game they even had a dog sled race! The main idea of the Olympics is: "The important thing is not winning, but taking part...".

1. **In the story, the word summer means:**
   a. a warm time of year
   b. a time when leaves fall
   c. a cold time of year

2. **Another word for event is:**
   a. food
   b. happening
   c. apples

3. **The opposite of strong is:**
   a. idea
   b. story
   c. weak

4. **A word in the story that sounds like witch is:**
   _____

5. **The word they stands for:**
   a. silver
   b. game
   c. Olympics

6. **A word in the story that goes with countries and states is:**
   a. cities
   b. sports
   c. races

★ On the back of this paper write about what sport you'd like to do in the Olympics.

Name _____

An Important Job

Do you know what Michael Collins did? <u>He</u> piloted the spacecraft **Columbia** that circled 69 miles above the moon. His fellow **astronauts**, Edwin Aldrin and Neil Armstrong, landed on the moon. Collins stayed in the spacecraft. For almost two days he flew around the moon. Armstrong and Aldrin explored below. Collins said he didn't mind being by himself. His job was important. Without him, no one could have returned!

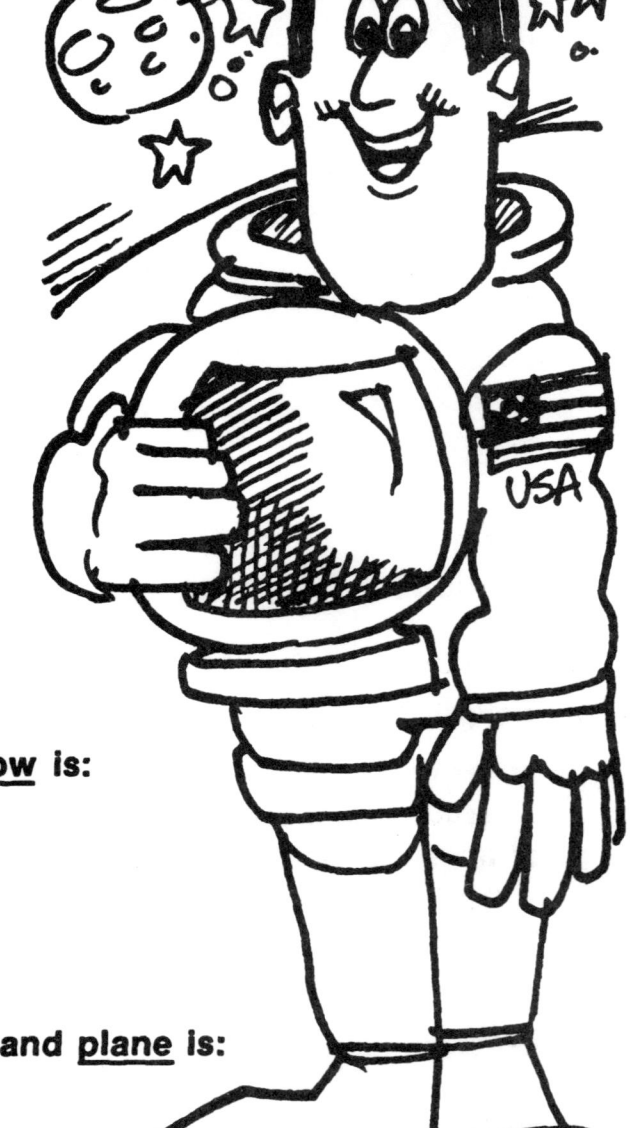

1. **In the story, the word <u>astronaut</u> means:**
   a. a person trained to drive a car
   b. a person who travels in space
   c. a person trained to ride a horse
2. **Another word for <u>alone</u> is:**
   a. together
   b. always
   c. single
3. **The opposite of <u>above</u> is:**
   a. below
   b. always
   c. never
4. **A word in the story that sounds like <u>know</u> is:**
   _____
5. **The word <u>he</u> stands for:**
   a. Edwin Aldrin
   b. Neil Armstrong
   c. Michael Collins
6. **A word in the story that goes with <u>train</u> and <u>plane</u> is:**
   a. spacecraft
   b. himself
   c. important

★ On the back of this paper make a list of things you'd like to take to the moon.

Name _____

A Hard Journey

Would you like to ride in a covered wagon for 2,000 miles? Pioneers who went west did just that. This five-month trip on a prairie **schooner** was very difficult. During rainy days children had to stay inside their small dark wagons. Clothing had to be washed in muddy rivers. **Fuel** had to be gathered for cookfires. <u>You</u> might have enjoyed the evening **fandangoes**. There you could dance to fiddle music and listen to stories. A warm fire might make you dream of home.

1. **In the story, the word <u>covered</u> means:**
   a. closed
   b. open
   c. only

2. **Another word for <u>like</u> is:**
   a. wash
   b. enjoy
   c. dark

3. **The opposite of <u>inside</u> is:**
   a. under
   b. over
   c. outside

4. **A word in the story that sounds like <u>mite</u> is:**
   _____

5. **The word <u>you</u> stands for:**
   a. children
   b. a person reading this story
   c. a great fire

6. **A word in the story that goes with <u>poems</u> and <u>tales</u> is:**
   a. dark
   b. rain
   c. stories

★ **On the back of this paper write two sentences about the way you travel. Draw a picture of yourself going on a trip.**

Name _____

Ancient Plants and Animals

Have you ever found a **fossil**? Often they are hard parts of animals that have turned to stone. The animal that owned the parts may have lived a billion years ago. Sometimes a whole animal is found. Insects trapped in sap from ancient trees look as they did when they lived. Larger animals were sometimes trapped in ice or tar. Some, frozen in ice, were so fresh when found that they have been eaten! Most museums have good fossil collections, but sometimes you can find your own. Hunt along the shore, in the mountains, near a road or even by the city.

1. **In the story, the word <u>fossil</u> means:**
    a. something warm
    b. a part of an ancient animal
    c. something cold

2. **Another word for <u>parts</u> is:**
    a. colors
    b. sounds
    c. pieces

3. **The opposite of <u>lived</u> is:**
    a. died
    b. played
    c. painted

4. **A word in the story that sounds like <u>rode</u> is:**
   _____

5. **The word <u>they</u> stands for:**
    a. ice
    b. tar
    c. fossils

6. **A word in the story that goes with <u>caught</u> and <u>held</u> is:**
    a. eaten
    b. trapped
    c. city

★ On the back of this paper write three sentences telling what you know about fossils.

Name _____

Some Uses For Sand

Have <u>you</u> enjoyed playing in the pale white sand of a beach? The pieces of sand come from rocks that are ground by wind and waves. Red sand and black sand can be found in different parts of **Hawaii**. The colors show that the sand was made from special rocks. There is sand by the sea, and by lakes and rivers. There are huge amounts in the deserts. Sand is used to make glass. Some is used to take dirt out of water. And some is used to make sandpaper. **Navajo** Indians make beautiful paintings with sand.

1. **In the story, the word <u>sand</u> means:**
   a. fine ground rock
   b. large stones
   c. paintings

2. **Another word for <u>beach</u> is:**
   a. grass
   b. shore
   c. yard

3. **The opposite of <u>beautiful</u> is:**
   a. ugly
   b. lovely
   c. clean

4. **A word in the story that sounds like <u>pail</u> is:**
   _____

5. **The word <u>you</u> stands for:**
   a. Indians
   b. the person reading this story
   c. people who make glass

6. **A word in the story that goes with <u>big</u> and <u>great</u> is:**
   a. glass
   b. sandpaper
   c. huge

★ **On the back of this paper write a story about what you do with sand when you go to the beach.**

Name _____

It Always Comes Back

Did you ever throw anything away that came back to you? A certain kind of **boomerang** can. It's a curved stick that tribes in **Australia** use for hunting and sport. A long piece of wood is bent after it has been boiled. When it is the right shape, it is held in place until dry. It is then tossed with a snap of the wrist. It will sail a long distance if it is thrown correctly. If the owner is skillful, <u>he</u> can use it again and again.

1. **In the story, the word <u>boomerang</u> means:**
    a. a straight stick
    b. a curved stick
    c. a distance

2. **Another word for <u>shape</u> is:**
    a. color
    b. feel
    c. form

3. **The opposite of <u>long</u> is:**
    a. short
    b. house
    c. late

4. **A word in the story that sounds like <u>sale</u> is:**
    _____

5. **The word <u>he</u> stands for:**
    a. the boomerang
    b. the owner
    c. the wrist

6. **A word in the story that goes with <u>fishing</u> and <u>trapping</u> is:**
    a. held
    b. Australia
    c. hunting

★ On the back of this paper write a story about "The Boomerang That Didn't Come Back."

Name _____

A Famous Uncle

Uncle Sam is recognized by most people right away. In his hat decorated with stars and his white beard, <u>he</u> stands for the U.S. government. Uncle Sam was never a real person. In 1812, the U.S. Army stamped its meat "U.S.". Someone thought that should mean "Uncle Sam". It started out as a joke, but later the U.S. government decided Uncle Sam should represent them. Uncle Sam appears on many posters printed by the government. In newspapers, artists use Sam to make **comments** about the country.

1. **In the story, the word <u>recognized</u> means:**
   a. known
   b. after
   c. hidden

2. **Another word for <u>real</u> is:**
   a. have
   b. give
   c. true

3. **The opposite of <u>many</u> is:**
   a. pull
   b. few
   c. more

4. **A word in the story that sounds like <u>write</u> is:**
   _____

5. **The word <u>he</u> stands for:**
   a. Uncle Sam
   b. meat
   c. the government

6. **A word in the story that goes with <u>fish</u> and <u>cheese</u> is:**
   a. stars
   b. meat
   c. think

★ On the back of this paper draw a picture of Uncle Sam. Write two sentences telling what you know about him.

Name _____

All This From a Tree!

Paper is made from trees that are chopped, cut into logs and ground. The ground **pulp** is treated in a special way. Threads from the wood are forced to separate from the rest. These threads are hooked onto one another. They are beaten, dried and pressed into smooth rolls. Paper is made into cereal boxes and school books, cups and tickets. It has been made into bathing suits and underwear. Every year, each of us uses over 400 pounds of paper. Can you imagine a world without paper?

1. **In the story, the word ground means:**
   a. changed to powder
   b. left alone
   c. blown away

2. **Another word for imagine is:**
   a. give
   b. think
   c. take

3. **The opposite of smooth is:**
   a. bright
   b. dull
   c. rough

4. **A word in the story that sounds like weigh is:**

   _____

5. **The word it stands for:**
   a. trees
   b. paper
   c. bathing suits

6. **A word in the story that goes with glasses and mugs is:**
   a. tickets
   b. books
   c. cups

★ On the back of this paper list things made of paper.

Name _____

All About Wasps

Wasps are insects with four clear wings and thin waists. <u>They</u> can be brown, black, red or blue and have colored stripes. Some wasps live alone and some live in large groups. Those who live in large groups make nests of paper. They chew dead wood and plants until they become ground up and sticky. They shape their balloon nests with this mixture. When it is dry it turns to a thin but strong paper. Queen wasps sting insects and spiders, but do not kill them. They are left for the wasp babies to eat when they hatch.

1. **In the story, the word <u>clear</u> means:**
    a. dark
    b. able to see through
    c. cloudy

2. **Another word for <u>thin</u> is:**
    a. fat
    b. hard
    c. slender

3. **The opposite of <u>alone</u> is:**
    a. together
    b. lonely
    c. left

4. **A word in the story that sounds like <u>wastes</u> is:**
    _____

5. **The word <u>they</u> stands for:**
    a. paper
    b. nests
    c. wasps

6. **A word in the story that goes with <u>ant</u> and <u>bee</u> is:**
    a. balloon
    b. wasps
    c. nests

★ **On the back of this paper write a story about the insect that you like best.**

Name _____

A Fast Game

Ice hockey is a very fast sport. <u>It</u> is played by six-person teams on a field of ice. There are three lines across the ice and a net at both ends. Each team tries to hit a small rubber **puck** into the opposite net. The players use long curved sticks and wear padded uniforms. Three players from each team protect their nets behind blue lines. The other three players from each team try to score points. Ice hockey is so fast, the players don't have time to turn around. They must learn to skate backward!

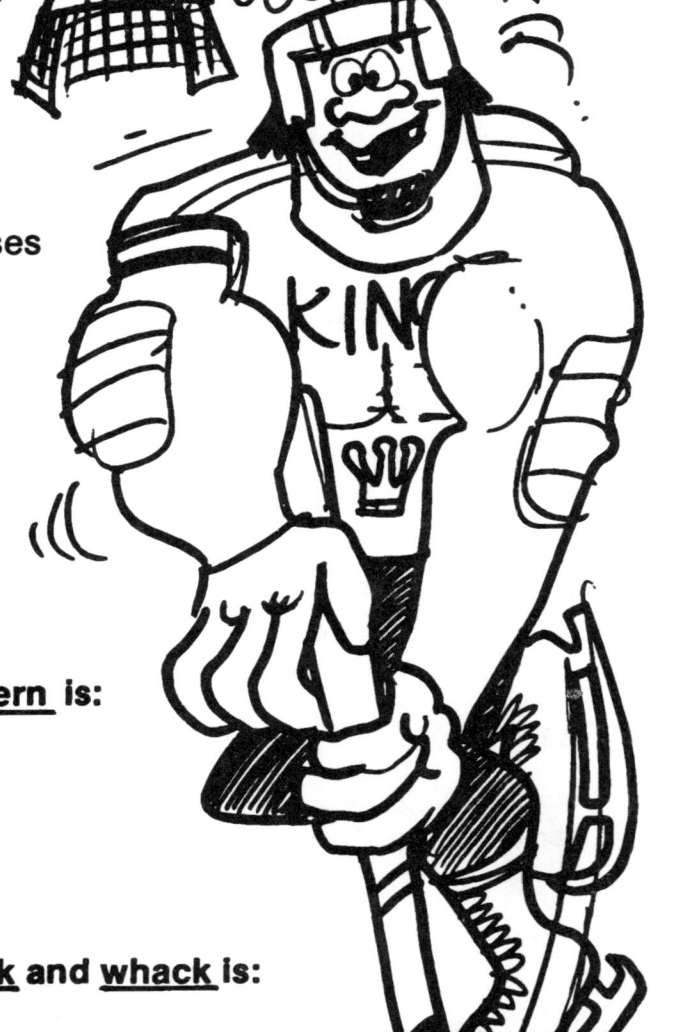

1. **In the story, the word <u>field</u> means:**
   a. a large area with buildings
   b. a large area without trees and houses
   c. a water-filled area

2. **Another word for <u>divides</u> is:**
   a. drives
   b. butters
   c. separates

3. **The opposite of <u>fast</u> is:**
   a. slow
   b. swift
   c. full

4. **A word in the story that sounds like <u>tern</u> is:**
   _____

5. **The word <u>it</u> stands for:**
   a. ice hockey
   b. field
   c. lines

6. **A word in the story that goes with <u>smack</u> and <u>whack</u> is:**
   a. players
   b. skate
   c. hit

★ **On the back of this paper write about the sport you play best. Tell why you like it and why you do it well.**

Name _____ Date _____

Mirror, Mirror On the Wall . . .

There are moustaches of every color, shape and size. Some people grow "handlebar" moustaches, which are long and curled at the ends. Masuriya Din, of India, decided to grow his marvelous moustache in 1949. By 1979, it had grown to the length of seven feet, ten inches!

Has your mother ever said, "Cut your nails! They're a sight!"? She wouldn't complain about you if she saw the nails of Mr. Chalil of India. The nails on his left hand haven't been cut since 1952. All together, they measure 100 inches long! They're all curled and curved, so they wouldn't be good for back-scratching.

Santa Claus has a pretty nice beard. So did Rip Van Winkle, who slept for twenty years. But in 1927, a man in Norway beat their beards easily. His was more than seventeen feet long!

Some ladies in Burma love necklaces. They wear so many of them that their necks slowly become stretched until they're fifteen inches long! They must wear their jewelry all their lives. If these copper coils are removed, the neck cannot hold the head up!

1. Who slept for twenty years?

2. What do some ladies in Burma love?

3. Where does the man with the beard live?

4. When did Mr. Din decide to grow his moustache?

5. Why don't Burmese women remove their necklaces?

6. How long are Mr. Chalil's nails?

Brainwork! Think about the question. Write the answer on the back. Make a list of all the bad and good things about having the world's longest nails.

The Long and the Short of It

Are there giants roaming the earth? You might think so if you went to China and met Miss Tseng. At seven feet, ten and one-half inches, she is believed to be the world's tallest female. Miss Tseng weighs 323 pounds. Miss Tseng has a good appetite. She eats twenty dumplings for breakfast and six bowls of rice at both lunch and dinner.

Over the years, many people have claimed to be taller than they really were. Some claimed to be ten feet tall! The tallest man in the world was really thought to have been Robert Wadlow, who lived from 1918 to 1940. Robert was eight feet, eleven inches tall! At the time of his death at the age of twenty-one, he was still growing!

A dwarf from India is the world's smallest adult. He is only twenty-eight inches tall! Dwarfs in the United States call themselves "little people". Some of them have been in movies and on television.

It's hard to be a giant. You really stand out in a crowd. Midgets and other tiny people don't have that problem. They have to be afraid of being crushed by a crowd.

1. Who was the world's tallest man?

2. What does Miss Tseng eat for breakfast?

3. Where would a giant really stand out?

4. When did Robert Wadlow die?

5. Why does Miss Tseng eat so much?

6. How do some dwarfs make a living?

Brainwork! Think about the question and answer it on the back. Write a paragraph about why you'd rather be a giant or a dwarf.

Fabulous Food

How about a piece of cherry pie? The largest cherry pie ever made weighed seven tons! In this huge pie were 4,950 pounds of cherries! It was made May 15, 1976 as part of the bicentennial celebration in a town in Michigan. How many pounds of pie do you think you could eat?

"I love hamburgers," said Gene. "I could eat the biggest hamburger in the world!" Tony smiled. "I bet you couldn't. The biggest one was made in Australia in 1975. It weighed 2,859 pounds!" Gene thought about that. "Well," he said, "then maybe I could eat the second biggest one!"

Do you ever get sick of eating ice cream? Never? Suppose you had been invited to eat the world's longest banana split. It measured 7,005 feet! It included 11,400 bananas, 1,500 gallons of ice cream and 250 pounds of chocolate!

How many people do you think it would take to eat the world's largest pizza? It was over 80 feet across, weighed 18,664 pounds and was cut into 60,318 slices!

1. Who thought he could eat a big hamburger?

2. What contained 11,400 bananas?

3. Where was the biggest burger made?

4. When was the biggest cherry pie made?

5. Why was the cherry pie made?

6. How was the biggest pizza served?

Brainwork! Think about the question and answer it on the back. What "biggest in the world" food would you like to make? What would you do with it?

Champion Moneymakers

"What are you going to be when you grow up?" Sylvia asked Linda. Linda thought. "Maybe I'll be a violinist," said Linda. "They don't make much money," declared Sylvia. "Well," replied Linda, "Fritz Kreisler was the highest paid violinist ever. He made more than two million dollars during his career."

"Big deal," laughed Sylvia. "Liberace, the pianist, earned more than two million dollars each year!" Hmmm, thought Linda. Perhaps I'd better switch from violin lessons to piano lessons.

The next day Sylvia saw Linda hitting a tennis ball against her garage door. "Why aren't you practicing to become a rich and famous pianist?" she asked. "Forget that!" Linda shouted. "Jimmy Connors once won 500,000 dollars for playing in one tennis match!"

"What are you going to be, Sylvia?" Linda asked. "I thought about being a boxer. In 1980, Sugar Ray Leonard lost his championship fight. He got paid 8,500,000 dollars and he lost! I don't really care about money. I just want to have fun and help people, too. I'm going to be a scientist."

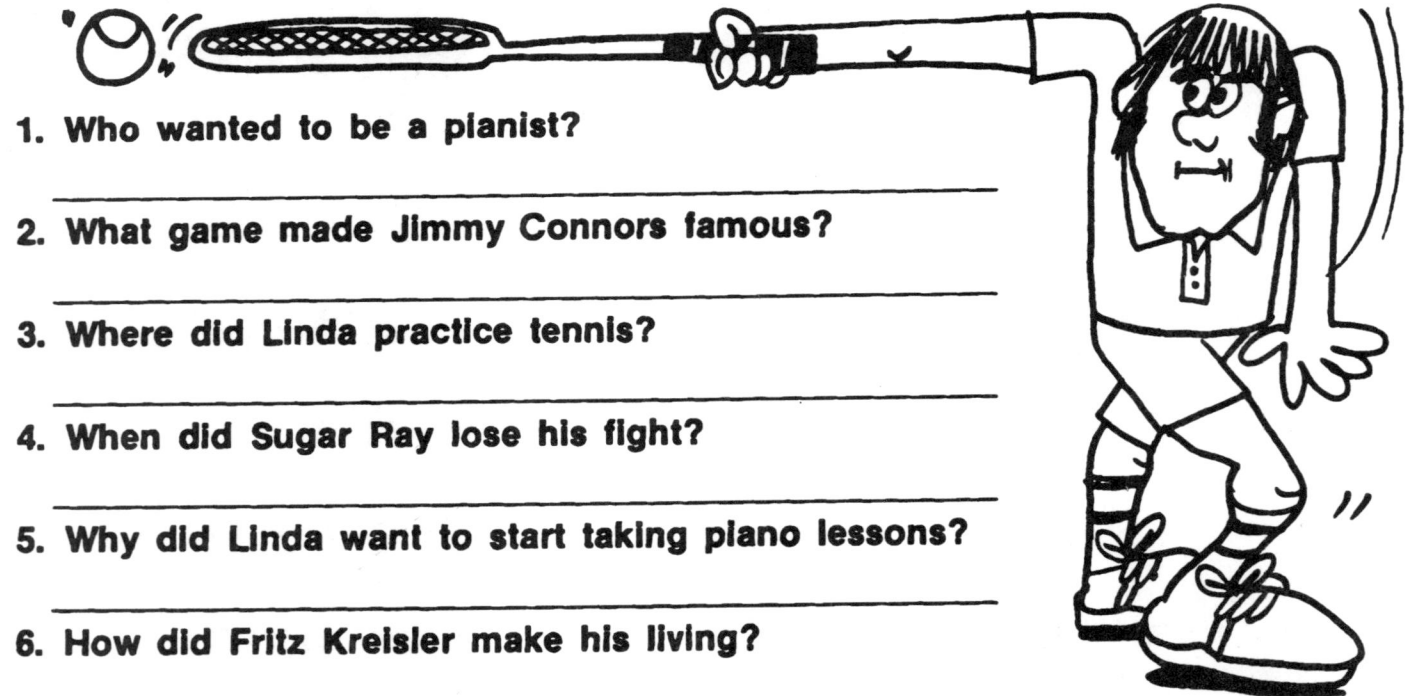

1. Who wanted to be a pianist?

2. What game made Jimmy Connors famous?

3. Where did Linda practice tennis?

4. When did Sugar Ray lose his fight?

5. Why did Linda want to start taking piano lessons?

6. How did Fritz Kreisler make his living?

Brainwork! Think about the question and answer it on the back. Write a paragraph about what you want to be and why.

Name _____ Date _____

Super Sports

Are you great at sports? Perhaps someday you'd like to be in the Olympics or be a professional athlete. If you're a basketball player, you have a good chance of winning on the United States Olympic team. Americans won all the gold medals in this game from 1936 to 1968. Then, they were beaten by the Russians, but regained their title in 1976.

Riding a bike is great fun. Going as fast as you can on a safe road can be thrilling. Maybe you can beat Dr. Allen Abbott's speed. He rode at 140.5 miles per hour behind a pace car in Utah in 1973. The car set the speed and Allen rode behind it for three-quarters of a mile.

In gymnastics, contestants from Eastern Europe are hard to beat. A girl from Czechoslovakia once won seven gold medals.

If you don't skate, it's hard to believe that someone can stand up and skate around on those thin blades. Eric Heiden of the United States not only can skate, he is the world's fastest skater. In the 1980 Olympics, Eric won five gold medals when he placed first in all the speed events!

1. Who is the world's fastest bike rider?
   _____

2. What did the American basketball team do in 1976?
   _____

3. Where do many great gymnasts live?
   _____

4. When did Eric Heiden win his gold medals?
   _____

5. Why does ice skating look hard to do?
   _____

6. How could you beat Dr. Abbott's record?
   _____

Brainwork! Think about the question and answer it on the back. Write a paragraph telling how you think an Olympic athlete trains to win.

Name _____ Date _____

Speedy Sports

Do you like speed and action? Do slow sports put you to sleep? Here's a sport that's just for you: skydiving! This sport of jumping out of airplanes is the world's fastest non-mechanical sport. You can fall at 185 miles per hour in a free fall. If you go up very very high, you can reach speeds of 614 miles per hour! Wait! Don't forget your parachute!

Maybe just talking about the world's fastest sport tired you out or even scared you. Think about trying the world's slowest sport: wrestling. Watching this sport can be a good way to catch up on some sleep. The holds can be so long, that one match took more than eleven hours!

The fastest car race in the world is the NASCAR. In 1970, William Yarborough's average speed for this race was more than 183 miles per hour!

Watch out for that hockey puck! The highest speed of that small round object was made by Bobby Hull. The puck whizzed by at 118.3 miles per hour!

1. Who made a hockey puck go fastest?
   _____
2. What is the world's fastest car race?
   _____
3. Where can you catch up on your sleep?
   _____
4. When did William Yarborough go his fastest?
   _____
5. Why might someone like skydiving?
   _____
6. Why is wrestling so slow?
   _____

Brainwork! Think about the question and answer it on the back. Would you like to skydive? Write a paragraph telling why or why not.

Can You Top This?

What do you have to do before you bake an apple pie? Peel the apples, of course! Kathy Wolfer of Wolcott, New York likes to peel apples in one long peel. In 1976 she took a twenty-ounce apple and peeled it. The unbroken peel was 172 feet, four inches long! It took Kathy eleven hours and 30 minutes to do it. It would take a long time to peel enough for a pie!

How long do you think you can stand on one foot? Try it at recess time. A man from Sri Lanka balanced himself on one foot for 33 hours!

If you can play an instrument well you can be proud of yourself. Rory Blackwell of England can play 75 instruments at once! All the instruments play the same tune. Rory must really be proud. He is a "one-man band".

Here's something you wouldn't want to try. Howard Davis of Somerset, England, had a "beard" made of bees! In 1952 Howard let about 20,000 bees swarm around his chest and throat. The stings of so many bees can kill. Believe it or not, not even one bee stung Howard!

1. Who is a "one-man band"?

2. What unusual thing did Howard Davis do?

3. Where did Rory Blackwell live?

4. When could you try standing on one foot?

5. Why didn't Howard die from bee stings?

6. How did Kathy peel her apple?

Brainwork! Think about the question and answer it on the back. Why did it take Kathy so long to peel one apple?

What Will They Do Next?

Mother couldn't believe it. Alison was making her bed without being told. In fact, she kept making it and unmaking it! "Alison, what on Earth are you doing?" asked her mother. "I'm trying to beat Wendy Wall's record," said Alison, out of breath by then. "She made a bed in 28.2 seconds." Hmm, Mother thought, I wonder if they have room-cleaning records, too.

When we see a performance we like, we often clap like crazy. A man in Sri Lanka just clapped to break a record. He clapped for 42 hours and six minutes in 1980. His average was 140 claps each minute!

A group of baton twirlers called the Havant Hurricanes twirled their batons for 55 hours! Not one of the six girls dropped her baton even once!

Here's a good way to draw people to your store. Barry Walls broke a record for non-stop lying on a bed of nails. Right in the window of a furniture store, he lay on that bed for 74 hours!

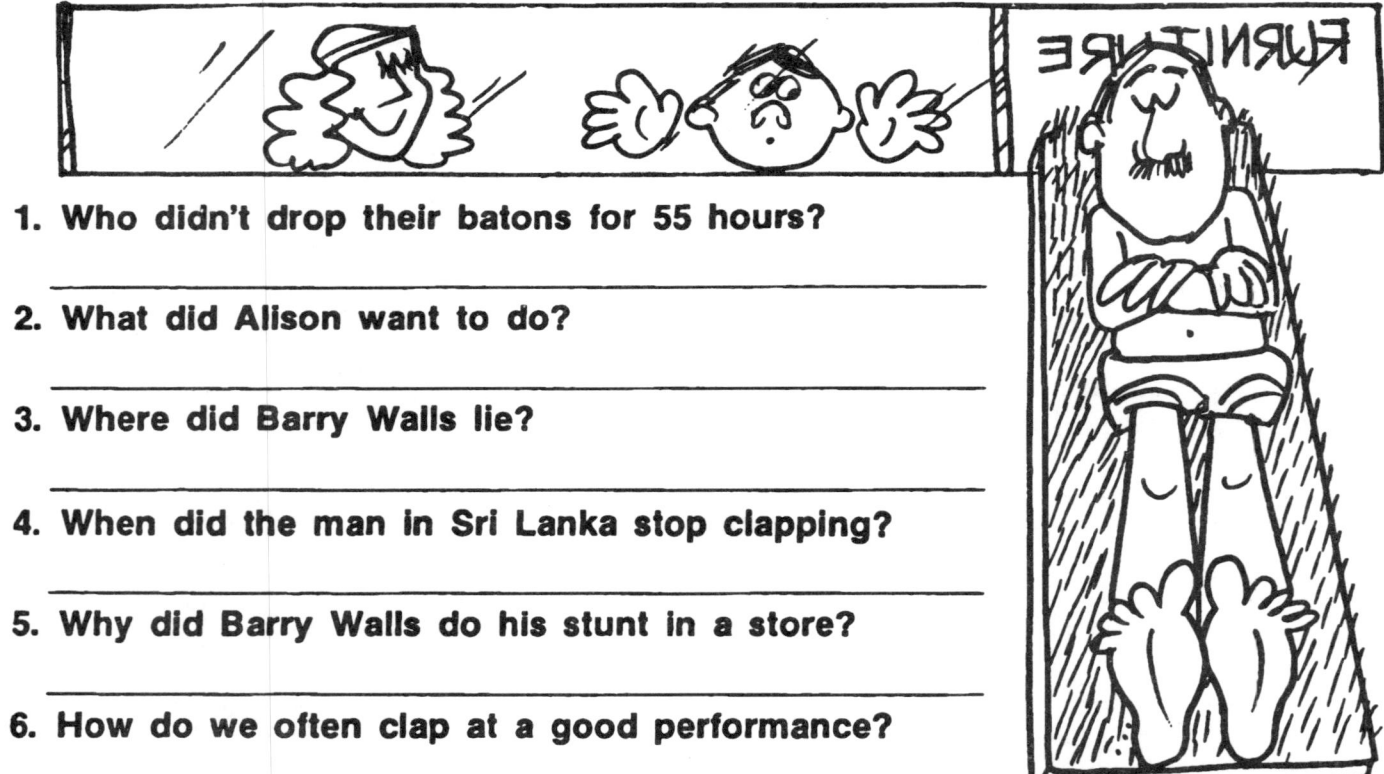

1. Who didn't drop their batons for 55 hours?

2. What did Alison want to do?

3. Where did Barry Walls lie?

4. When did the man in Sri Lanka stop clapping?

5. Why did Barry Walls do his stunt in a store?

6. How do we often clap at a good performance?

Brainwork! Think about the question and answer it on the back. What kind of record would your mother like you to break?

Hard Work!

Do you have a yo-yo gathering dust in your closet? The popularity of yo-yos comes and goes. They really caught on in 1926, when Mr. Duncan started a yo-yo factory. Most yo-yos made today are Duncan yo-yos. In 1977 John Winslow of Virginia worked his yo-yo for 120 hours! Take your yo-yo out of that closet. Maybe you can beat John's record!

Anyone can take long walks on their feet. It takes more skill, though, to walk a long distance on your hands. Way back in 1900 Johann Hurlinger of Austria walked 10 hours each day for 55 days—completely on his hands. When he quit he'd walked 871 miles, from Vienna, Austria to Paris, France.

Have you ever heard someone yodel? You have to train your voice to sing those tricky up and down notes. The champion yodeler is Errol Bird of Ireland. He yodeled for ten hours, fifteen minutes without stopping!

Richard Baterip of England can clean three regular size office windows in record time—48 seconds! Richard did this in the yearly Top Shiner contest in England. That made him the Top Shiner of all!

1. Who walked from Vienna to Paris?

2. What difficult thing can Errol Bird do?

3. Where should you look for your old yo-yo?

4. When did yo-yos become popular?

5. Why was Johann's walk unusual?

6. How did Richard Baterip become Top Shiner?

Brainwork! Think about the question and answer it on the back. Which one of the stunts above do you think you could do best? Why?

Down on the Farm

Masaryktown, Florida has an unusual kind of contest— for chicken pluckers! In 1976, a team of four women plucked twelve chickens clean in 32.9 seconds! In this contest, if even one feather is left on a chicken, everyone yells, "Fowl!"

Most cows are milked by machine nowadays. On small farms, however, milking is still done by hand. The milking record was set a long time ago. In 1937, Andy Faust of Oklahoma milked for twelve hours straight. He got 120 gallons of milk for his hard work!

Do you like cheese? The French are the biggest cheese eaters in the whole world. Speaking of cheese, the biggest cheese wheel ever made was a giant cheddar cheese weighing 34,591 pounds! It was driven from Wisconsin to the New York World's Fair in 1964 in a special vehicle called a "Cheese Mobile".

Maybe your nice warm wool sweater came from a sheep sheared by G. Phillips. He sheared 694 lambs in nine hours! Mr. Phillips set this record in Wales on June 25, 1975.

1. Who eats the most cheese in the world?

2. What happens if feathers are left on plucked chickens?

3. Where might your wool sweater come from?

4. When did Mr. Phillips set his record?

5. Why was a "Cheese Mobile" necessary?

6. How are most cows milked?

Brainwork! Think about the question and answer it on the back. The word "fowl" is a homonym for "foul". Write the meanings of both words.

Name _____ Date _____

Something to Sneeze About and Other Stories

Sam sneezed eight times in a row. "You must be getting a cold," said his sister. "So far, I have nothing to worry about," said Sam. "A girl in England caught a cold. She sneezed for 194 days without stopping. Finally, the doctors were able to stop it. I still have 193 days to go! Aaaa, aaaa, achoo!"

Hiccups are hard to stop. Someone can try to scare you out of them, or tell you to drink ten gulps of water really fast.

"Really, Don, you don't have to yawn while I'm talking to you," said Myra. "Am I boring you?" Don smiled. "No, but I wonder if a woman I heard about was bored. She yawned without stopping for five weeks straight!"

"Marty!" yelled Mrs. McFeeny. "Go to sleep!" Marty lay in bed thinking, I'm not sleepy. I hope I won't be like the man who lived until he was 94. He never slept a wink in his life! Zzzzzzzzzzzzzzzzzz.

1. Who was getting a cold?

2. What was Marty having trouble doing?

3. Where did the champion sneezer live?

4. How long did a woman yawn?

5. Why did Myra think Don was yawning?

6. How did the girl in England start sneezing?

Brainwork! Think about the question and answer it on the back. Write about all the ways you know for stopping hiccups.

Exciting Exercises

Are you physically fit? Do you bulge or have any blubber? You need exercise even if you are skinny. Exercise keeps your heart fit, too. It makes you feel better. You could start with some chin-ups. Use both hands, because only one person in 100,000 can do chin-ups with only one hand. In 1976, William Vaught did twenty one-handed chin-ups.

Sit-ups are great for your tummy muscles. How many can you do? Just lie down, put your hands behind your head, and start sitting up. Someone may have to hold your legs down. By the way, a man in California did 26,000 sit-ups in 11 hours and 44 minutes in 1977!

You have to have strong arms to do lots of push-ups. Tommy Gildert of England did 9,105 push-ups without stopping! It took him 4 hours, 17 minutes and 9 seconds! Wow!

Who jumps rope? Kids and boxers, right? Jumping rope is really great exercise at any age. Katsumi Suzuki of Japan jumped rope for 9 hours and 46 minutes nonstop in 1980!

1. Who holds the record for push-ups?

2. What do you need to do lots of push-ups?

3. Where was the sit-up record set?

4. When did William Vaught do twenty chin-ups?

5. How long did Mr. Suzuki jump rope?

6. How can you start your sit-ups?

Brainwork! Think about the question and answer it on the back. How do you do your favorite exercise? Write directions so someone else can try it.

Answer Key

Answer Key

Page 5

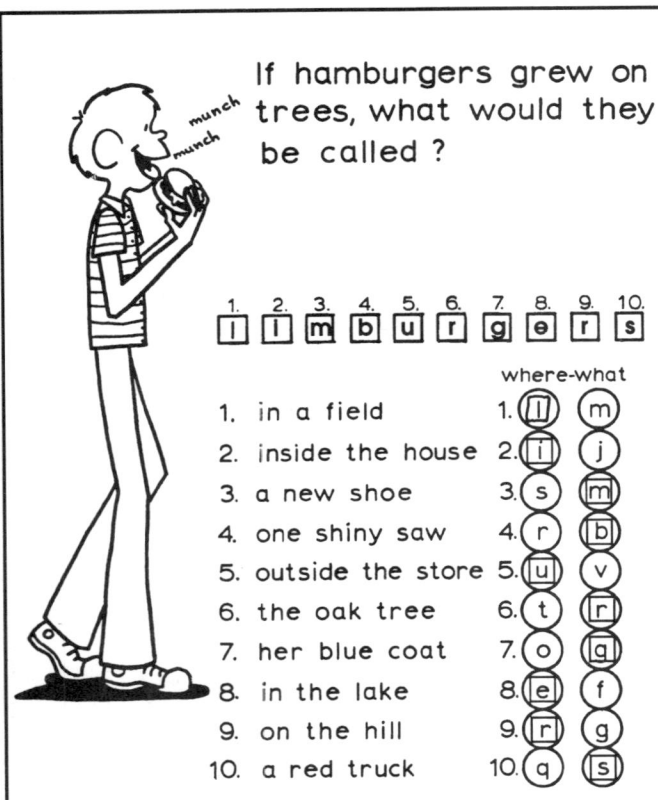

Page 7

What does a duck do when he flies upside down?

he quacks up
1 2 3 4 5 6 7 8 9 10

	what	when
1. airplanes	h	g
2. an apple tree	e	f
3. in the morning	d	q
4. a field of hay	u	v
5. at sunset	x	a
6. next week	m	c
7. a yellow basket	k	n
8. never again	r	s
9. at noon	t	u
10. closed the gate	p	w

Page 6

Page 8

Answer Key

Page 9

Page 10

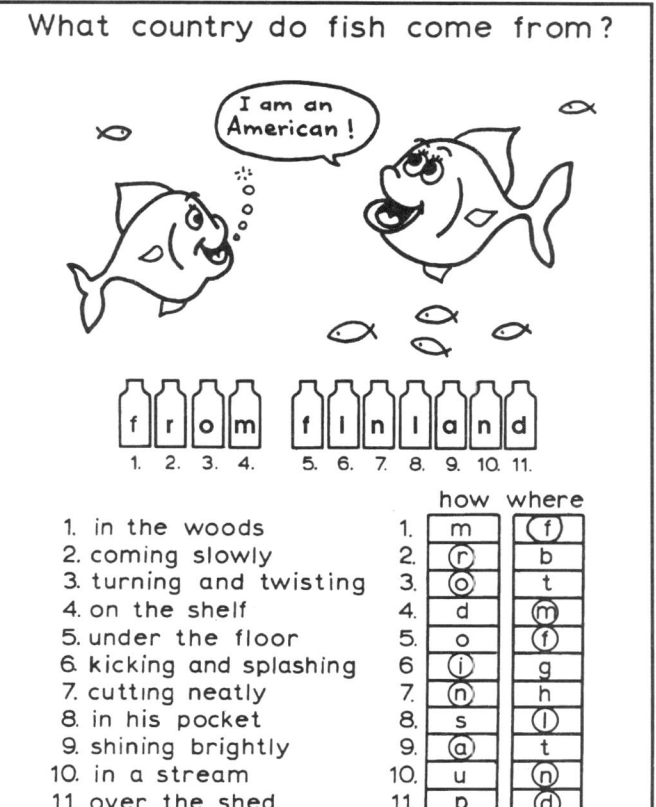

Page 11

Page 12

Answer Key

Page 13

What is the smallest bridge in the world?

The bridge [o][f] [y][o][u][r] [n][o][s][e]
1. 2. 3. 4. 5. 6. 7. 8. 9. 10.

	what	when	where
1. a buzzing bee	1. (o)	a	i
2. before the rain	2. g	(f)	h
3. in a little while	3. x	(y)	z
4. under the log	4. m	n	(o)
5. the blue lake	5. (u)	s	t
6. over the trees	6. q	d	(r)
7. on the boat	7. p	l	(n)
8. a green coat	8. (o)	r	t
9. after sunset	9. u	(s)	v
10. thunder clouds	10. (e)	w	x

Page 14

What two keys are too big to carry in your pocket?

m-o-n-k-e-y and d-o-n-k-e-y
1. 2. 3. 4. 5. 6. 7. 8. 9. 10. 11. 12.

	when	where	why
1. on Monday afternoon	1. (m)	n	o
2. asked him to come	2. p	q	(o)
3. behind her chair	3. r	(n)	s
4. all that day	4. (k)	l	h
5. around the house	5. f	(e)	g
6. to open that box	6. w	x	(y)
7. because the wind blew	7. b	c	(d)
8. under all the sand	8. r	(o)	s
9. late that night	9. (n)	u	x
10. in a far off time	10. (k)	h	j
11. high in a tree	11. g	(e)	m
12. for the wind was cold	12. n	s	(y)

Page 15

What is bought by the yard and worn by the foot?

[t][h][e] [c][a][r][p][e][t]
1 2 3 4 5 6 7 8 9

	where	why	how
1. because he was happy	1. r	(t)	s
2. on the roof	2. (h)	g	k
3. jumped quickly	3. f	a	(e)
4. because the storm came	4. b	(c)	d
5. climbing carefully	5. l	m	(a)
6. under the hill	6. (r)	u	y
7. he slid to a stop	7. x	n	(p)
8. for they were lost	8. j	(e)	u
9. in the bookshelf	9. (t)	z	m

Page 16

What's another name for a spot remover?

A d-o-g-c-a-t-c-h-e-r
1. 2. 3. 4. 5. 6. 7. 8. 9. 10.

	who	what	when	where
1. strawberries	1. (c)	(d)	e	f
2. by the door	2. (m)	n	p	(o)
3. four girls	3. (g)	h	k	l
4. yesterday	4. (a)	b	(c)	d
5. his uncle	5. (a)	f	t	u
6. a green basket	6. q	(t)	r	s
7. to the store	7. u	v	w	(c)
8. on the floor	8. x	y	n	(h)
9. in April	9. (h)	o	(e)	l
10. his brother	10. (r)	k	g	h

Answer Key

Page 17

Page 18

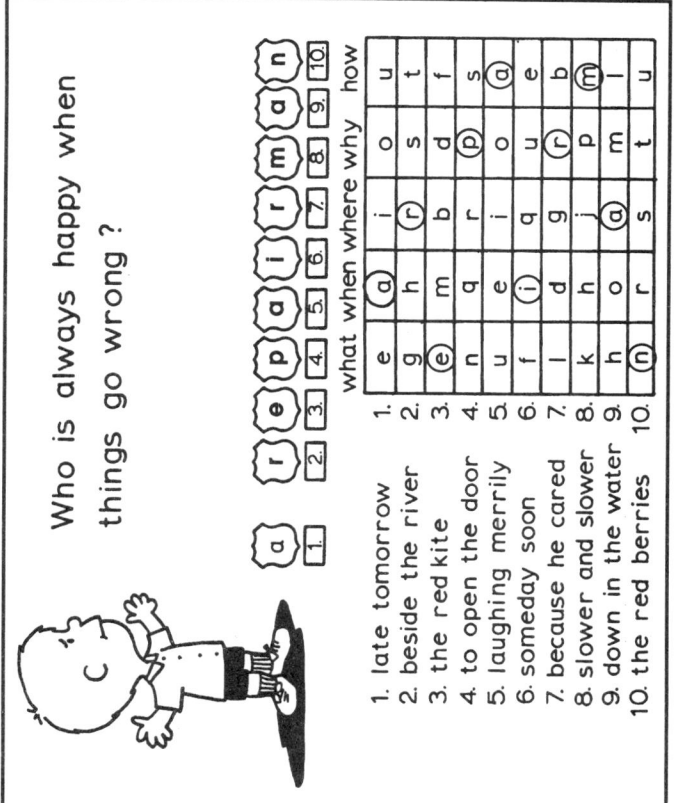

Page 19

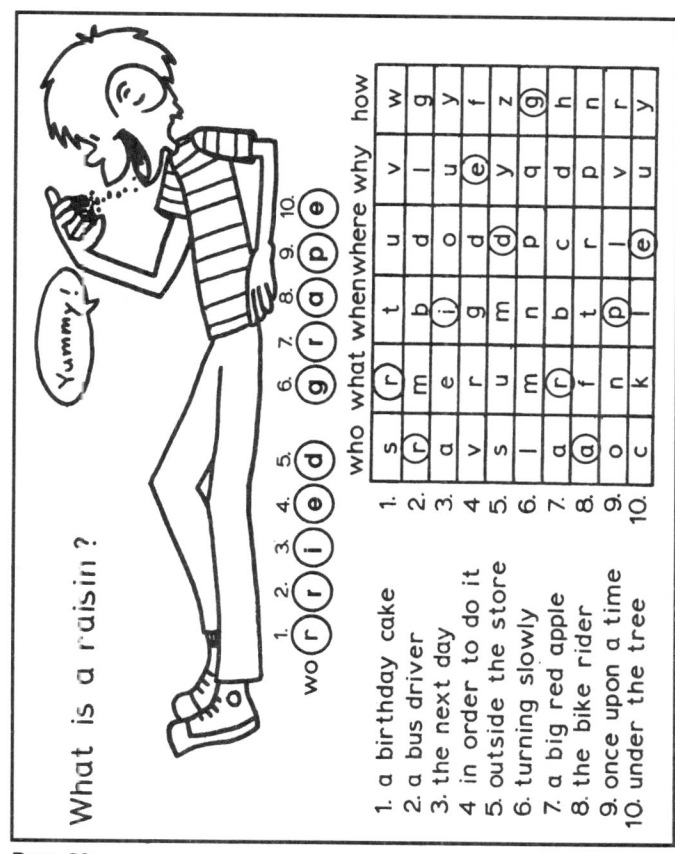

Page 20

Answer Key

Page 21

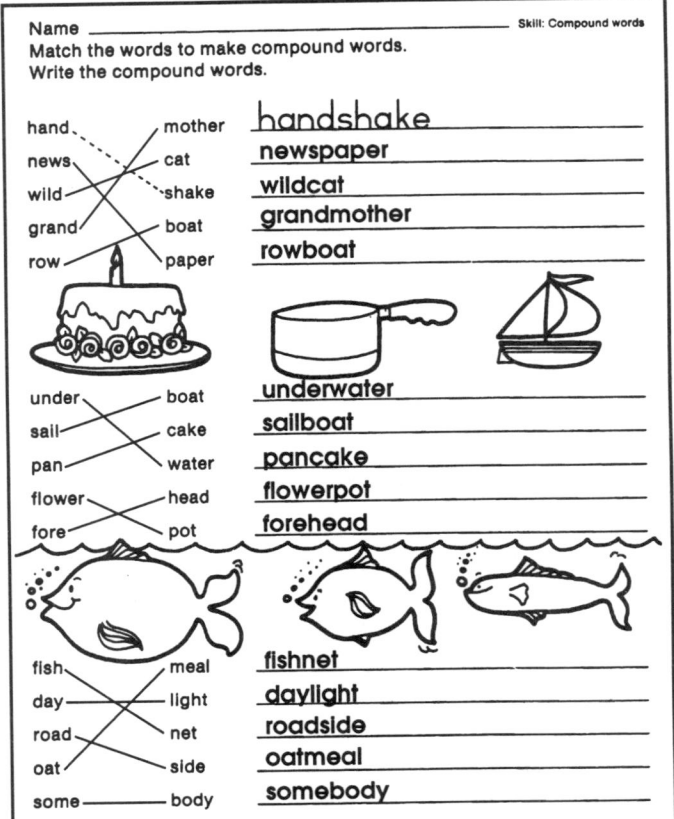

Page 22

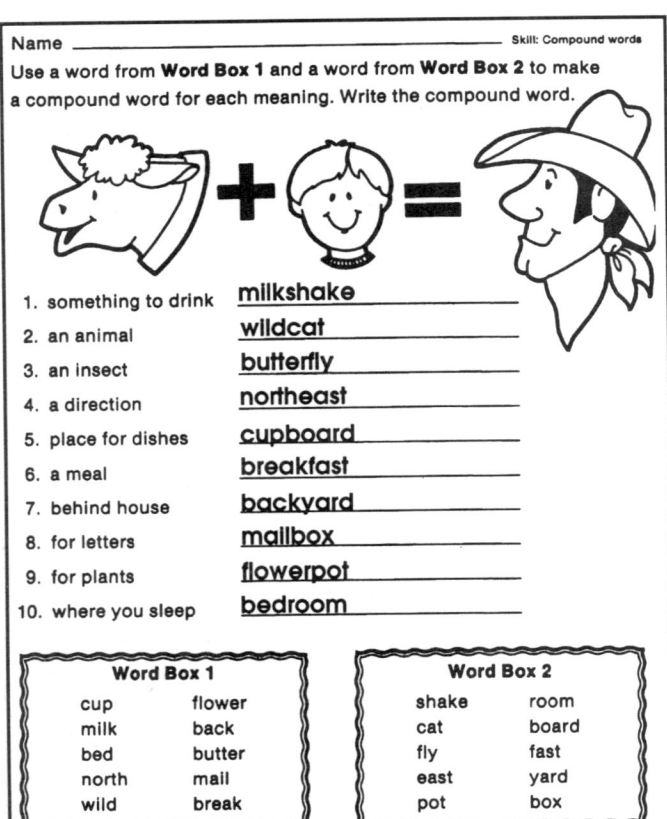

Page 23

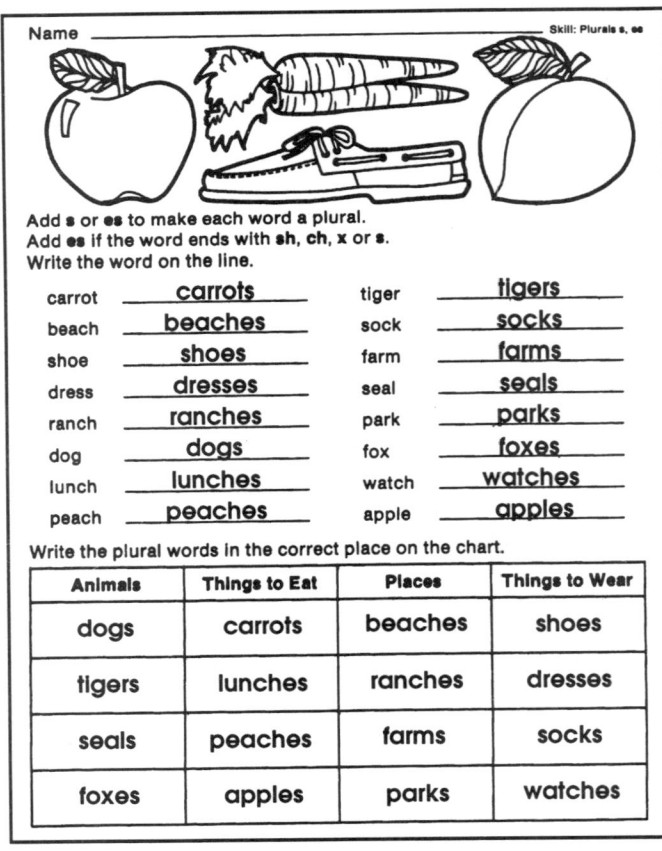

Page 24

Answer Key

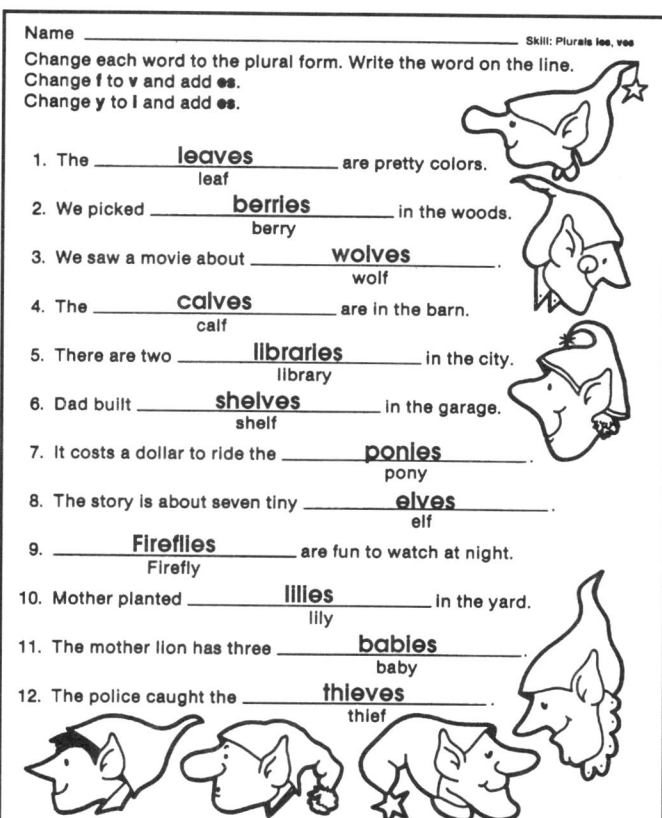

Page 25

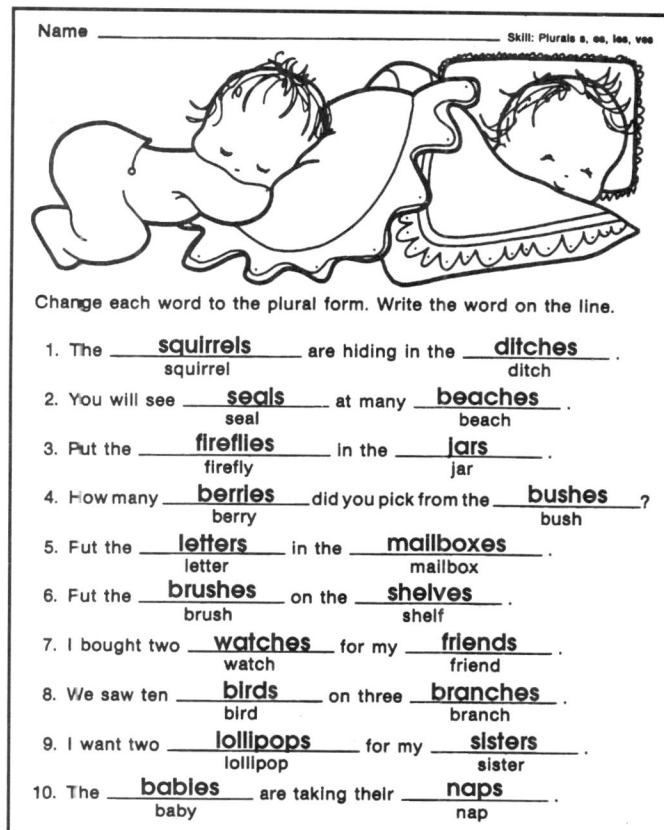

Page 26

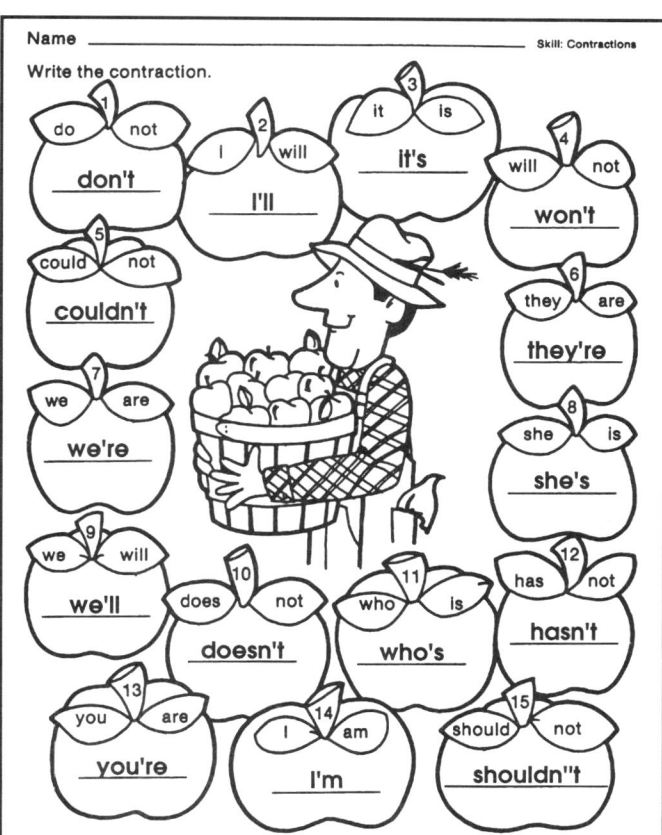

Page 27

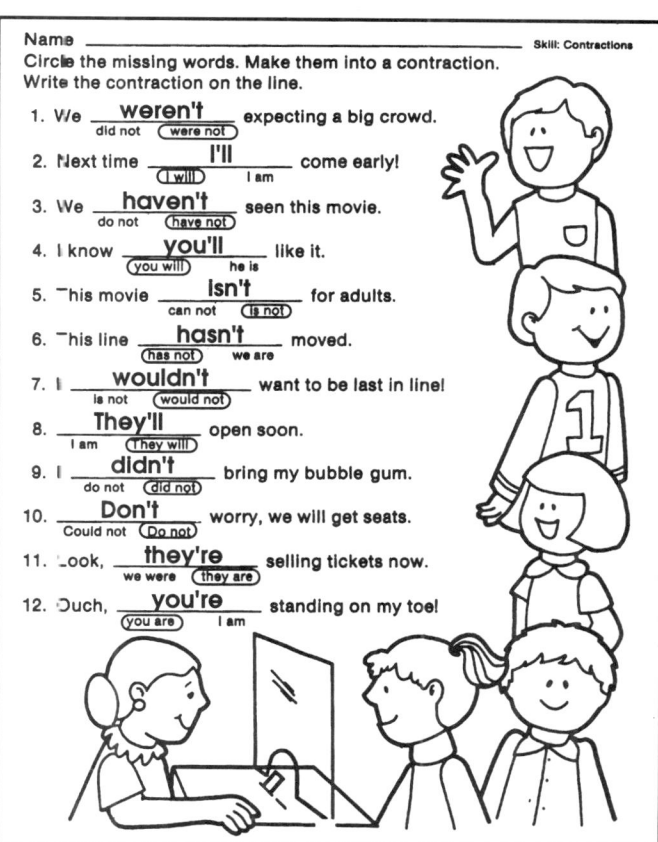

Page 28

Answer Key

Page 29

Skill: Possessives, Contractions for Is

Sam's dog is big. ('s shows possession)
Sam's late today. ('s shows a contraction for is)

Make a ✓ to show what 's stands for.

	possession	is
1. Sam's late today.		✓
2. Where is Mike's house?	✓	
3. Kim's going to camp.		✓
4. Is that Jane's kitten?	✓	
5. Mother's going to be here soon.		✓
6. The newspaper's late today.		✓
7. Put the teacher's papers on his desk.	✓	
8. Show me the baby's room.	✓	
9. Dad's car won't start!	✓	
10. The bell's going to ring.		✓
11. Today is Matt's birthday.	✓	
12. The door's unlocked.		✓
13. Where is the dog's bone?	✓	
14. The baby's sleeping now.		✓
15. The puppy's hungry.		✓

Write a sentence using 's to show possession.
Answers will vary.
Write a sentence using 's as a contraction for is.

Page 30

Skill: Possessives

Fill in the missing words.

Meet our family. Toto is my dog. My cat is named Silky.

Mr. Bumble | Mrs. Bumble | Scott | Toto | Sara | Silky

1. Sara is **Scott's** sister.
2. Toto is **Scott's** dog.
3. Mrs. Bumble is **Mr. Bumble's** wife.
4. Scott is **Sara's** brother.
5. **Sara's** cat is named Silky.
6. Mr. Bumble is **Mrs. Bumble's** husband.
7. Scott and Sara are Mr. and Mrs. **Bumble's** children.
8. Mr. and Mrs. Bumble are Scott and **Sara's** parents.

Page 31

Skill: Synonyms

Add a synonym to each.

Word Box: yell, under, small, smile, sick, big, close, help, start, stay, shy, talk, stop, hurry, fix

1. timid — **shy**
2. large — **big**
3. rush — **hurry**
4. ill — **sick**
5. tiny — **small**
6. repair — **fix**
7. scream — **yell**
8. begin — **start**
9. grin — **smile**
10. aid — **help**
11. remain — **stay**
12. below — **under**
13. halt — **stop**
14. speak — **talk**
15. shut — **close**

Page 32

Skill: Synonyms

Circle a synonym for the underlined word. Write another synonym from the Word Box on the line.

1. intelligent — (bright) friendly — **smart**
2. assist — repair (aid) — **help**
3. frigid — (chilly) weather — **cold**
4. puzzled — mean (baffled) — **confused**
5. bravery — (boldness) frighten — **courage**
6. dangerous — huge (hazardous) — **risky**
7. easy — careful (uncomplicated) — **simple**
8. trade — (exchange) buy — **swap**
9. repair — sell (mend) — **fix**
10. happiness — (joy) smile — **gladness**
11. calm — (quiet) pretty — **peace**
12. power — loud (strength) — **force**

Word Box: gladness, courage, simple, help, risky, confused, fix, swap, smart, force, cold, peace

Answer Key

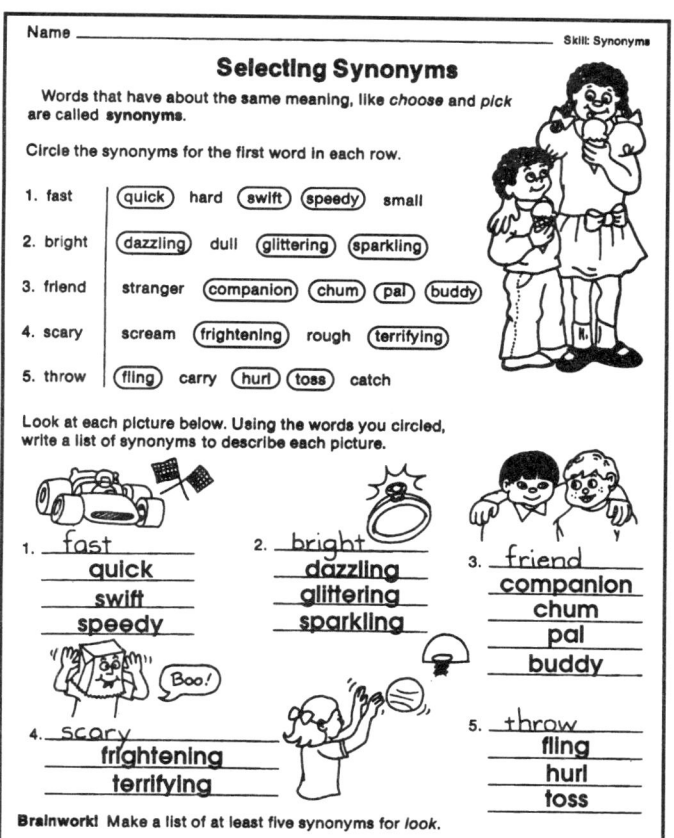

Page 33

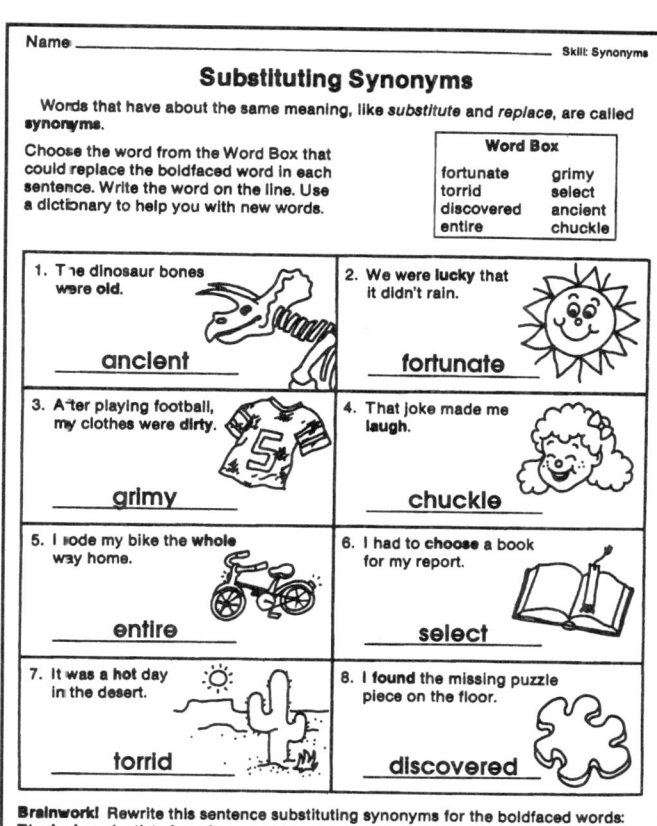

Page 34

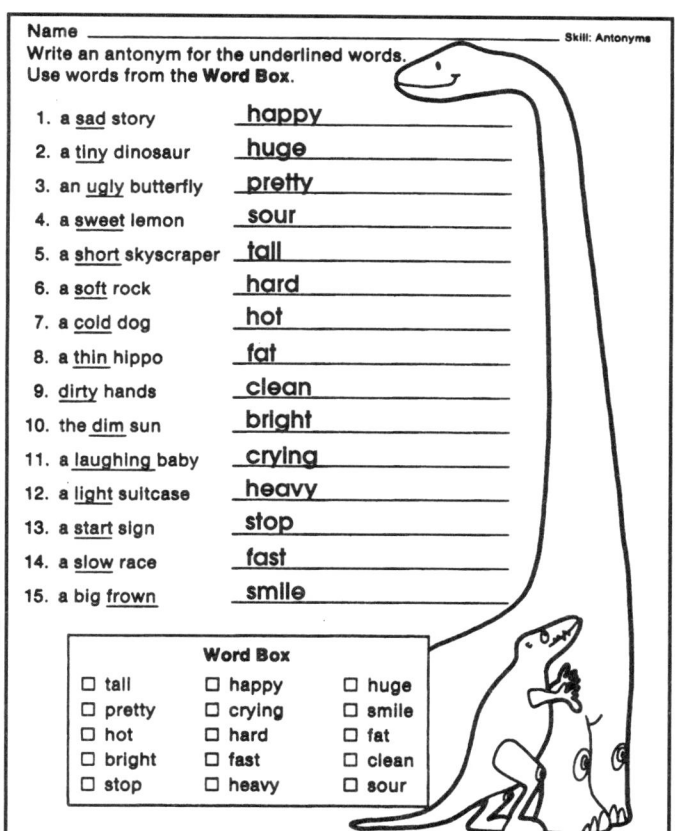

Page 35

Page 36

Answer Key

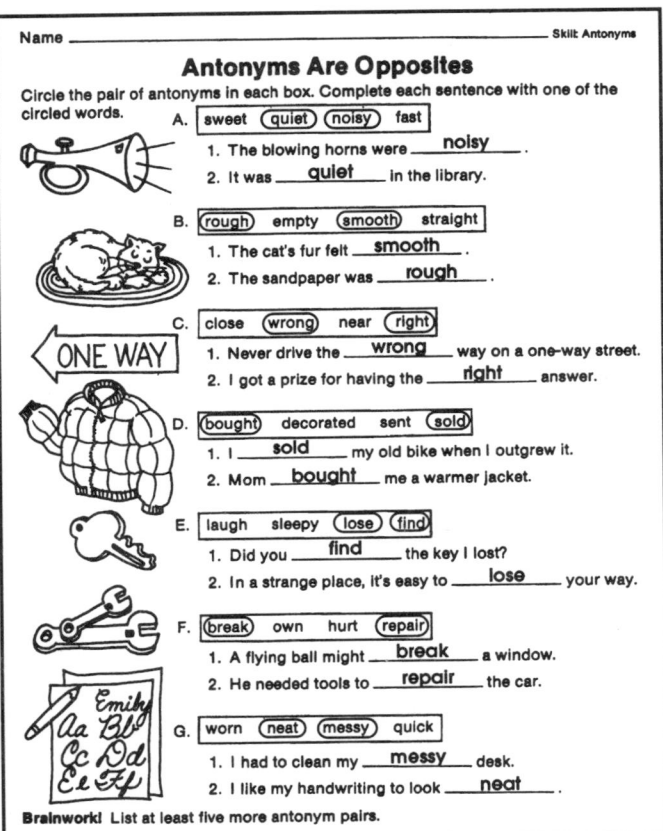

Page 37

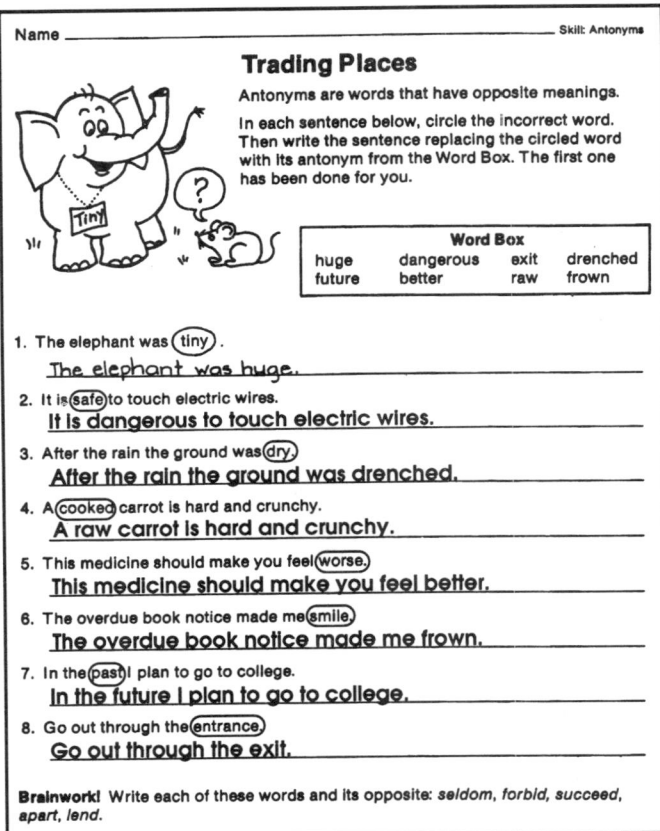

Page 38

Page 39

Page 40

Answer Key

Page 41

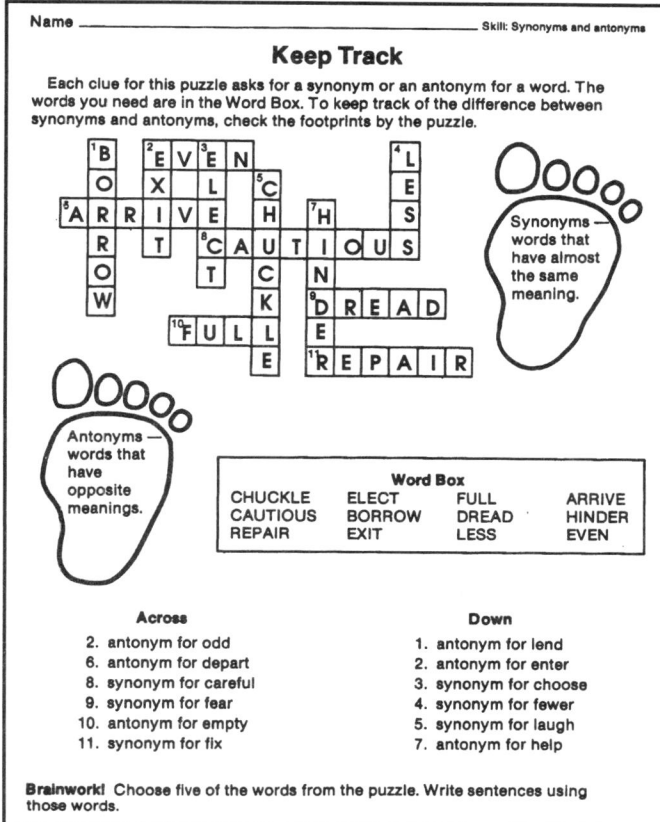

Page 42

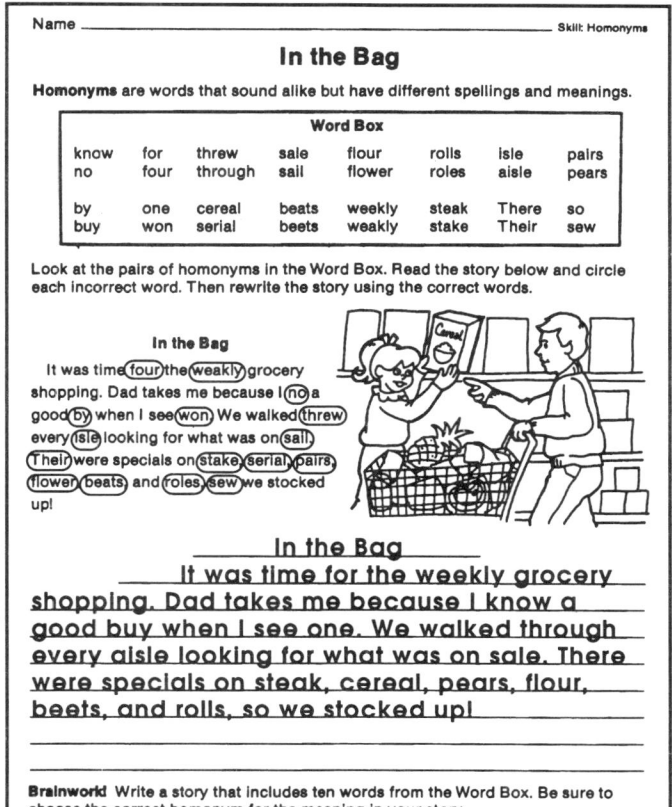

Page 43

Page 44

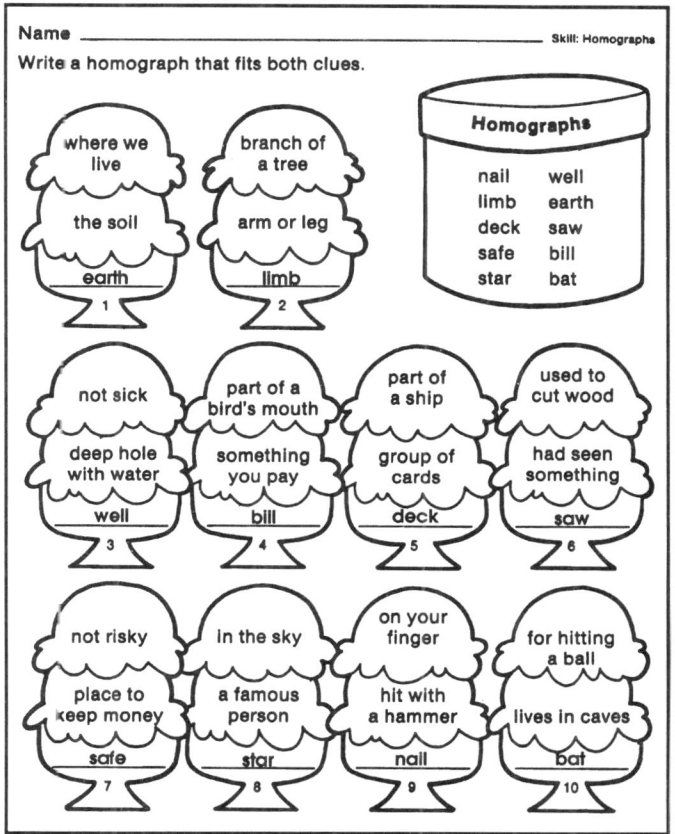

Answer Key

Page 45

Page 46

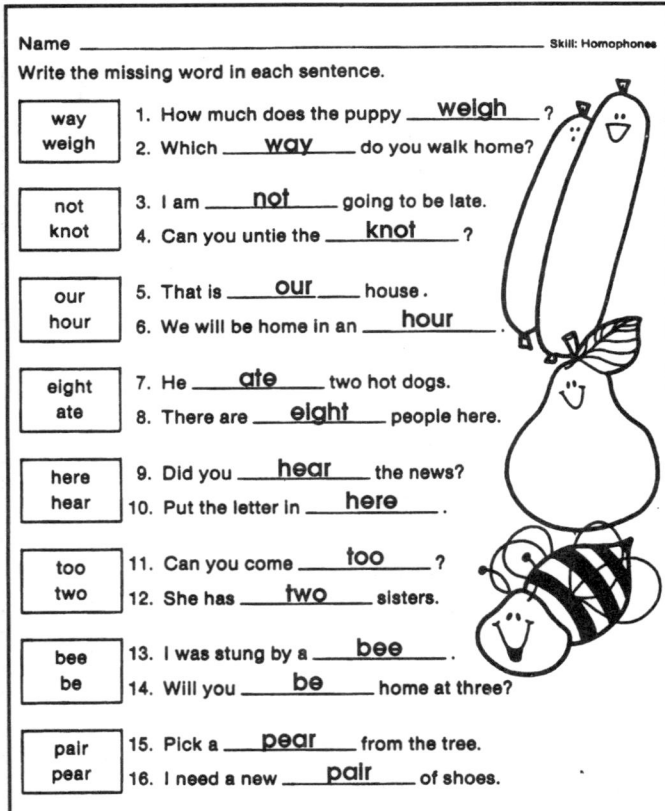

Page 47

Page 48

Answer Key

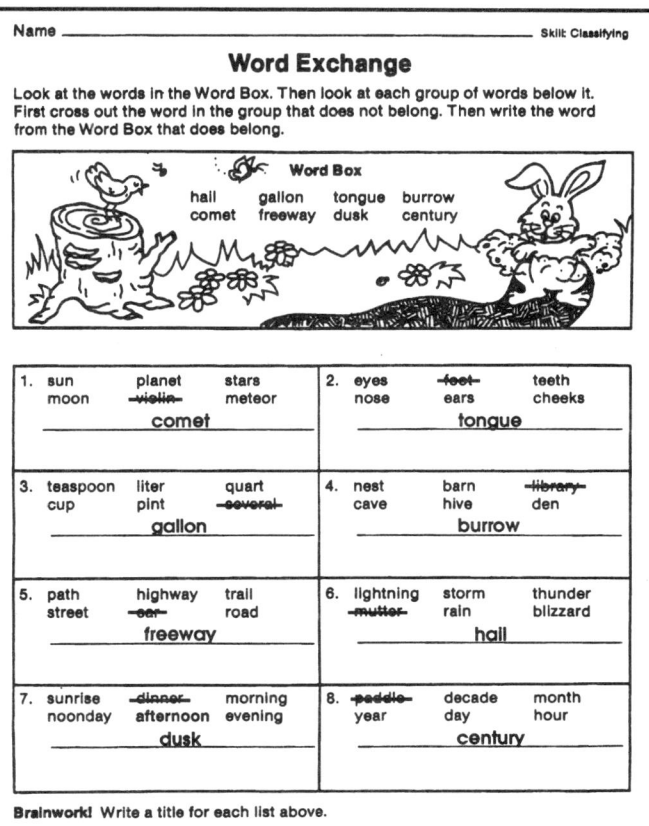

Page 49

Page 50

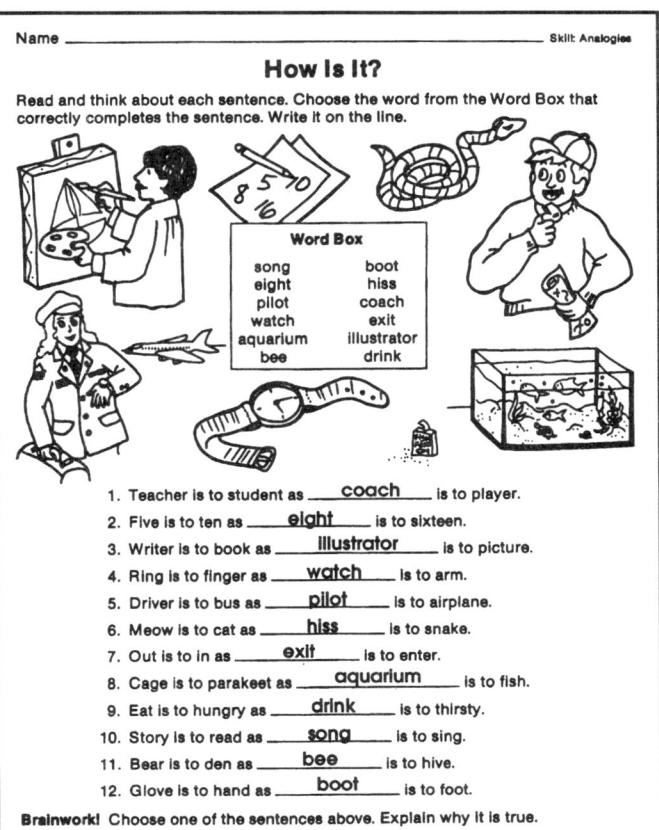

Page 51

Page 52

Answer Key

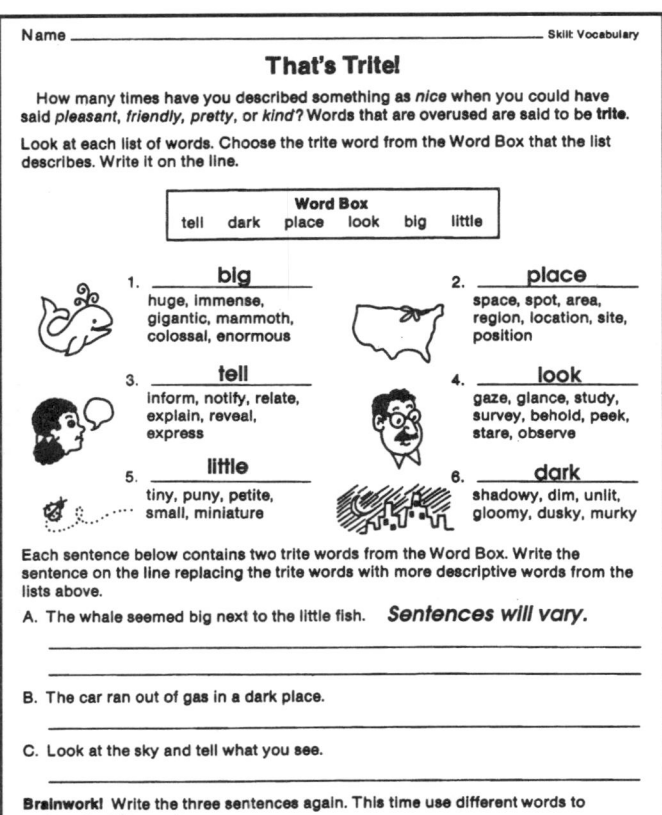

Page 53

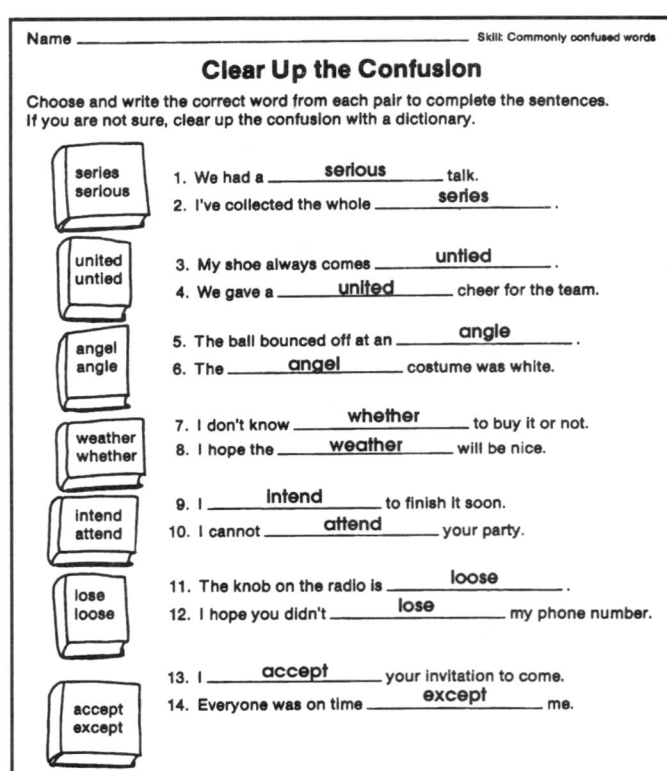

Page 54

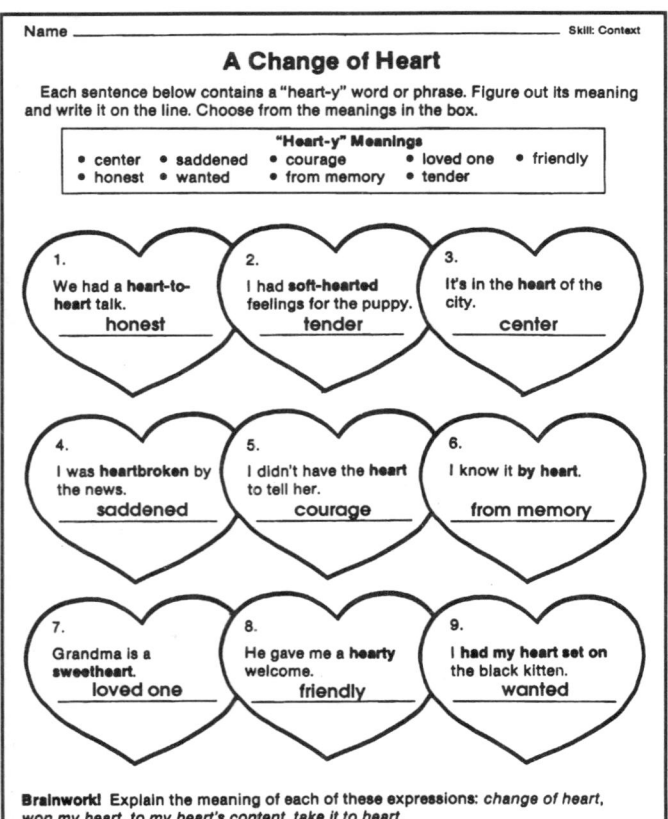

Page 55

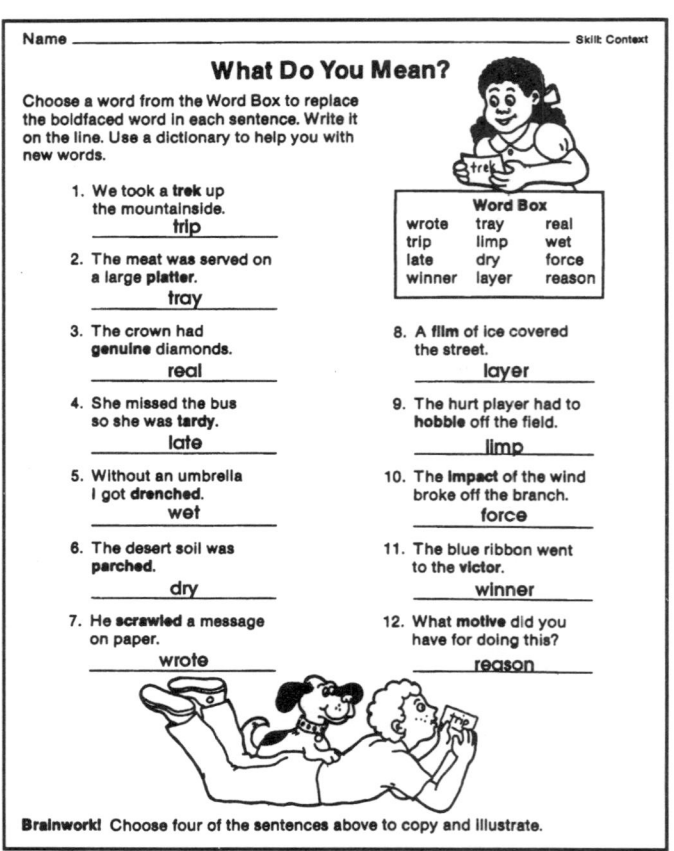

Page 56

Answer Key

Page 57 — Stay Tuned! (Skill: Getting meaning from context)

The name *television* comes from *tele-* meaning *far* in Greek, and *videre* meaning *to see* in Latin. Before 1950, the use of television was **rare**. Then, during a single **decade**, the ten-year period from 1950 to 1960, television became a part of almost every household in the United States. It **swiftly** became a **major** influence in people's lives. It changed the way they spent their time and let them see a whole new world right in their own homes.

Since the 1950s television has **evolved**, or grown and changed, to include uses in businesses, hospitals, schools, and law enforcement. As well as providing entertainment, television broadcasts business meetings and **monitors** hospital patients. It lets students study and observe world **events** as they happen, and even guards banks and prisons.

1. Which boldfaced word in the story means:
   a. a ten-year period? **decade**
   b. quickly? **swiftly**
   c. important? **major**
   d. grown and changed? **evolved**
   e. watches over? **monitors**
   f. happenings? **events**
   g. uncommon? **rare**

2. Where did the name for television come from?
   The name for television comes from tele meaning far in Greek, and videre meaning to see in Latin.

3. How did television influence people's lives after 1950?
   Answers will vary.

4. What do you think is television's most important use and why?
   Answers will vary.

Brainwork! Tell about one important world event that millions of people witnessed on television.

Page 58 — Volcanoes! (Skill: Scientific vocabulary)

Volcanoes are special kinds of mountains. Under volcanoes, deep in the earth, is a layer of hot, liquid rock called **magma**. Volcanoes are formed when the magma is suddenly forced up through a crack in the **crust**, or surface, of the earth. This action, called **eruption**, spills the hot magma, or lava, out onto the crust. As it cools, it hardens and forms mounds.

Scientists classify volcanoes in three groups. The first group includes volcanoes that have not erupted in hundreds of years. These volcanoes are **extinct** and are unlikely to erupt again. The second group also includes volcanoes that have not erupted in many years but these volcanoes are thought to be capable of erupting again. These volcanoes are called **dormant**. The final group includes volcanoes that erupted not long ago and could erupt again at any time. These volcanoes are said to be **active**.

Find and write a boldfaced word from the story for each description.
1. **magma** — liquid rock beneath the earth
2. **extinct** — group of volcanoes unlikely to erupt
3. **crust** — the outer surface of the earth
4. **eruption** — action that forces magma through the crust
5. **active** — group of volcanoes that have recently erupted
6. **dormant** — group of volcanoes that have not erupted in many years but still may erupt

Brainwork! Mount St. Helens in the state of Washington erupted on May 18, 1980. Find out about that event. Write your findings.

Page 59 — Computer Data (Skill: Technical vocabulary)

Computers may seem "smart" but they cannot think. The only thing they can do is follow a set of instructions called a **program** which must be written by a person. The computer **hardware** (machinery) and **software** (programs) work together.

For the computer to work, a person must enter **data**, or information, into the computer. This is called **input**. New data is entered by typing on a **keyboard** that has letters and symbols like a typewriter. Data may be stored on a **disk** which is used to record and save information.

Next, the computer "reads" the data and follows the instructions of the program. The program may tell it to organize the data, compare it to other data, or store it for later use. This is called data **processing**.

When the processing is complete, the computer can display the results either on the screen or printed on paper as a **printout**.

Find and write a boldfaced word from the story for each description.
1. **disk** — used to save and record information
2. **processing** — organizing, comparing, or storing data
3. **printout** — results printed on paper
4. **program** — set of instructions for a computer
5. **hardware** — computer machinery
6. **input** — entering data
7. **software** — computer programs
8. **keyboard** — where data is entered

Label each picture below **hardware** or **software**.

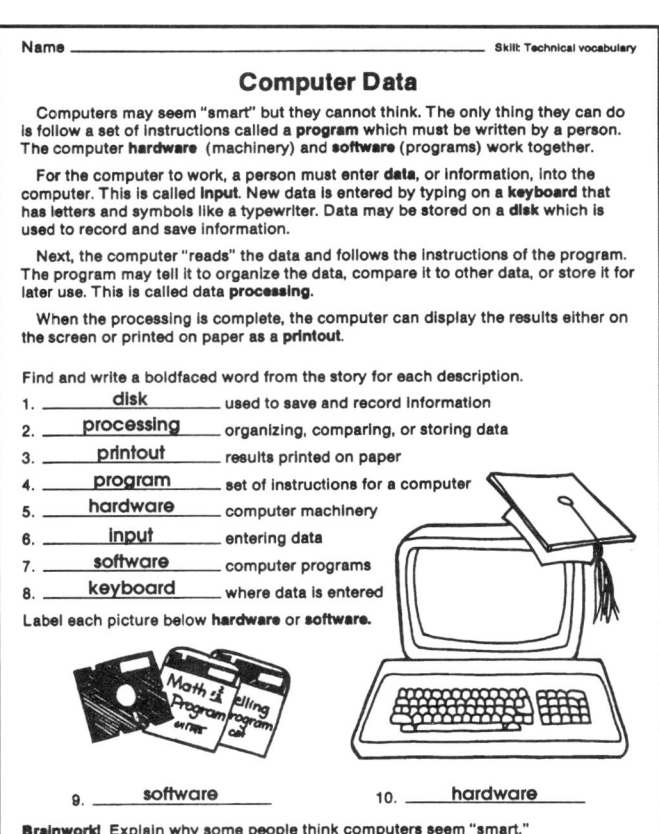

9. **software**   10. **hardware**

Brainwork! Explain why some people think computers seem "smart."

Page 60 — Words From Latin (Skill: Latin prefixes)

Some English words are made with prefixes borrowed from Latin.

Use the meanings of the Latin prefixes in the Word Box to help you write the English word for each definition below.

Word Box		
com- = together	semi- = half; partly	dis- = opposite
pre- = before	re- = back; again	sub- = below

1. a half circle — **semicircle**
2. below freezing — **subfreezing**
3. heat again — **reheat**
4. view before — **preview**
5. opposite of agree — **disagree**
6. write again — **rewrite**
7. gain back — **regain**
8. below soil — **subsoil**
9. partial darkness — **semidarkness**
10. press together — **compress**
11. opposite of honest — **dishonest**
12. appear again — **reappear**
13. opposite of respect — **disrespect**
14. partly automatic — **semiautomatic**

Brainwork! English borrows parts of words from Greek, too. The prefix *tele-* means *far*. Write five words you know that begin with *tele-*. Then write their meanings.

Answer Key

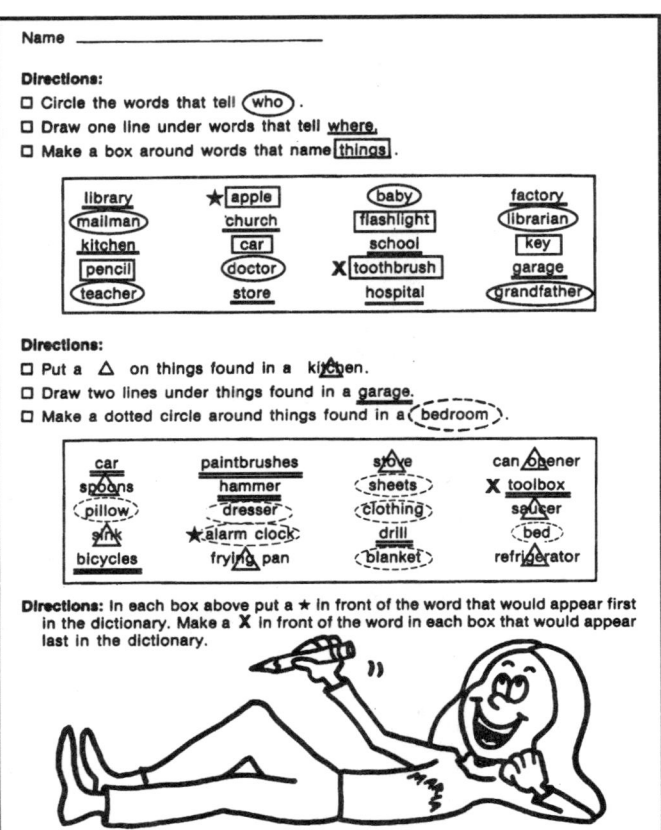

Page 61

Page 62

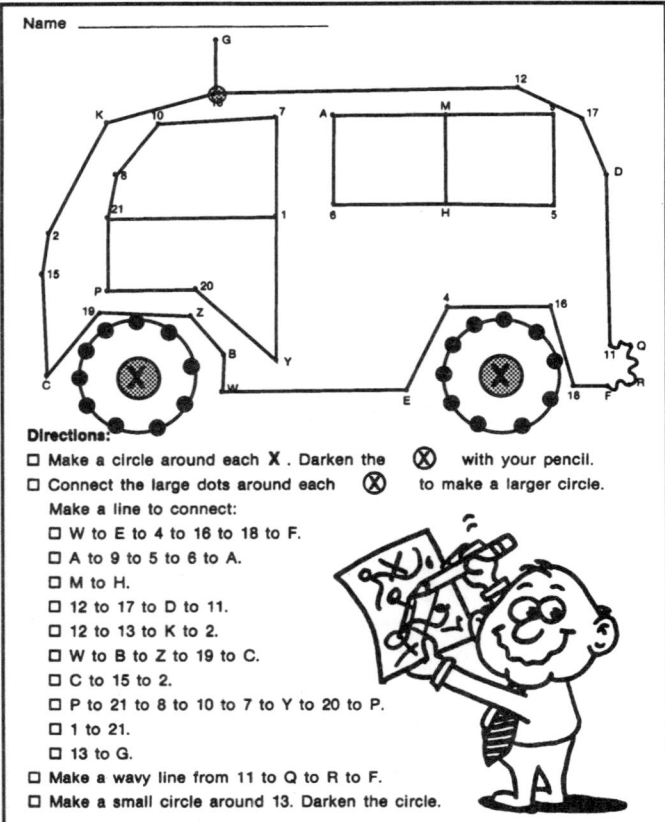

Page 63

Page 64

Answer Key

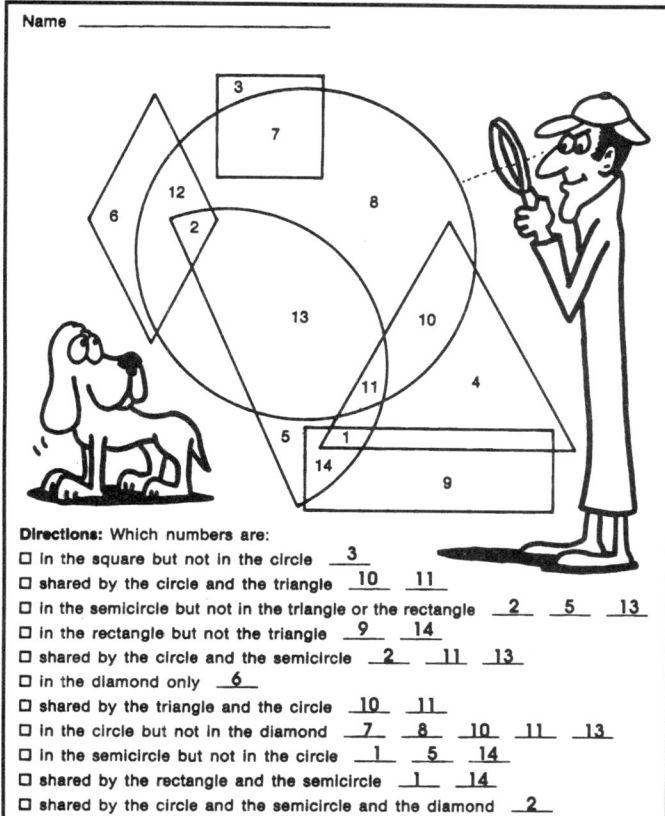

Answer Key

Page 69

Directions: Follow the directions below each grid. Count across, then up and make a dot for each pair of numbers. Connect the dots in the order you made them on the grid.

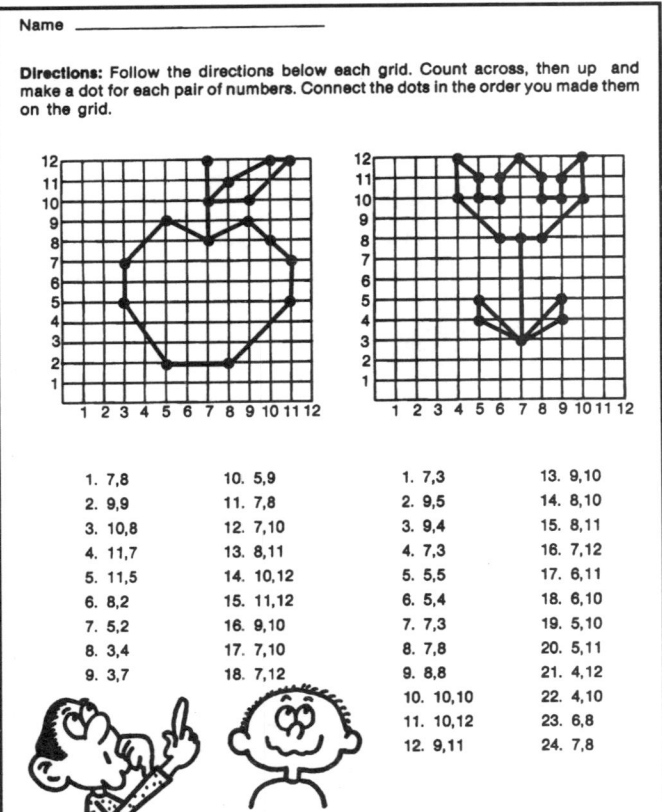

1. 7,8	10. 5,9	1. 7,3	13. 9,10
2. 9,9	11. 7,8	2. 9,5	14. 8,10
3. 10,8	12. 7,10	3. 9,4	15. 8,11
4. 11,7	13. 8,11	4. 7,3	16. 7,12
5. 11,5	14. 10,12	5. 5,5	17. 6,11
6. 8,2	15. 11,12	6. 5,4	18. 6,10
7. 5,2	16. 9,10	7. 7,3	19. 5,10
8. 3,4	17. 7,10	8. 7,8	20. 5,11
9. 3,7	18. 7,12	9. 8,8	21. 4,12
		10. 10,10	22. 4,10
		11. 10,12	23. 6,8
		12. 9,11	24. 7,8

Page 70

Directions: Magic Math Squares add up to the same number when you add across or down the rows.
☐ Find the solution for each math problem and write it in the answer column.
☐ Write the answers in the Magic ×÷ Square.

Box	Problem	Answer
☐ Q	36 ÷ 6	6
☐ P	21 ÷ 7	3
☐ B	18 ÷ 9	2
☐ X	32 ÷ 4	8
☐ D	8 × 0	0
☐ N	16 ÷ 2	8
☐ R	6 × 0	0
☐ T	24 ÷ 6	4
☐ S	16 ÷ 4	4
☐ C	3 × 6	18
☐ W	20 ÷ 10	2
☐ O	3 × 7	21
☐ A	30 ÷ 5	6
☐ Y	27 ÷ 9	3
☐ Z	2 × 8 + 1	17
☐ M	2 × 9	18

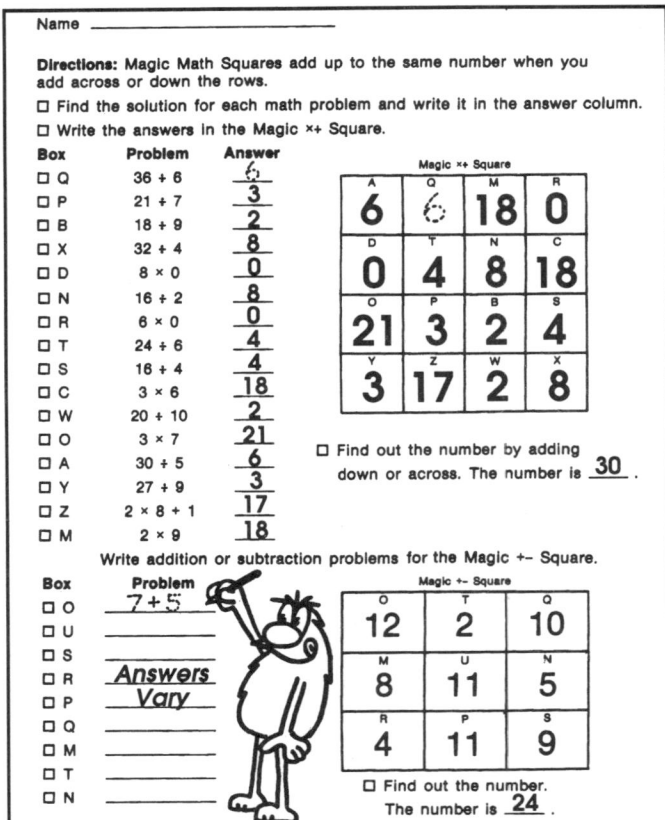

☐ Find out the number by adding down or across. The number is **30**.

Write addition or subtraction problems for the Magic +– Square.

Box	Problem
☐ O	7 + 5
☐ U	
☐ S	
☐ R	Answers
☐ P	Vary
☐ Q	
☐ M	
☐ T	
☐ N	

☐ Find out the number. The number is **24**.

Page 71

Directions: At the bottom of the page:
☐ On line 18 write the letter below the Ukulele.
☐ On line 4 write the letter above the Violin.
☐ Write the letter on the Classical Guitar on line 3.
☐ Write the letter below the Violin on line 1.
☐ Write the letter between the Cello and Mandolin on line 9.
☐ On line 8 write the letter above the Banjo.
☐ On line 15 write the letter between the Violin and Ukulele.
☐ Write the letter on the Cello on line 16.
☐ On line 10 write the letter below the Banjo.
☐ Write the letter above the Ukulele on line 14.
☐ On line 19 write the letter on the Banjo.
☐ On line 2 write the letter between the Banjo and Classical Guitar.
☐ Write the letter above the Cello on line 6.
☐ Write the letter on the Violin on line 13.
☐ On line 12 write the letter between the Mandolin and Classical Guitar.
☐ Write the letter between the Violin and Banjo on line 17.
☐ On line 5 write the letter above the Mandolin.
☐ Write the letter below the Cello on line 11.
☐ On line 7 write the letter below the Mandolin.

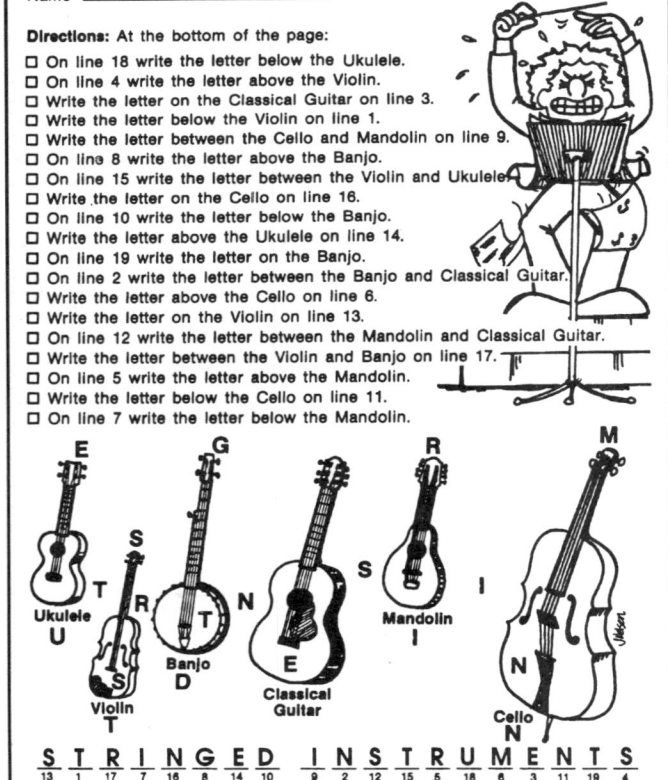

S T R I N G E D I N S T R U M E N T S
13 1 18 7 16 8 14 2 6   9 2 15 5 3 10 11 19 4

Page 72

Directions: Read the clues and write a word from the list. Then write the letters on the correct line in the Mystery Saying Box. The mystery saying was made up by Benjamin Franklin.

Clues

☐ a kind of plant — h o l l y
☐ opposite of night — d a y
☐ 365 days — y e a r
☐ opposite of love — h a t e
☐ group of people — t e a m
☐ kind of flower — r o s e
☐ opposite of us — t h e m

☐ opposite of lower — r a i s e
☐ a rule — l a w
☐ opposite of good — b a d
☐ very small — t i n y
☐ opposite of sleep — w a k e
☐ part of a camera — l e n s

Word List

holly	rose	year	hate
them	lens	law	tiny
raise	wake	team	bad
day			

Mystery Saying Box

E a r l y t o b e d.
E a r l y t o r i s e.
M a k e s a m a n h e a l t h y,
w e a l t h y a n d w i s e.

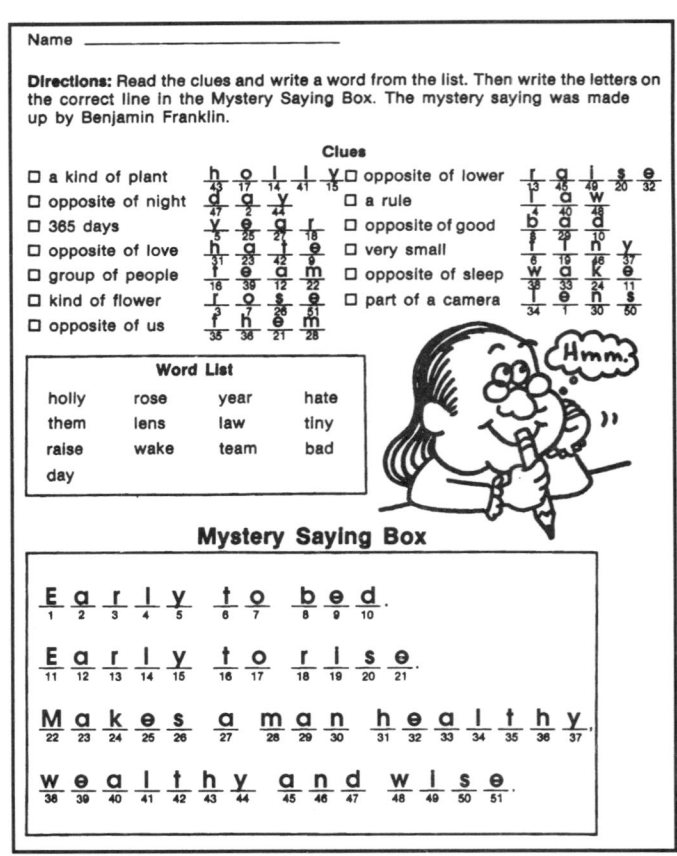

Answer Key

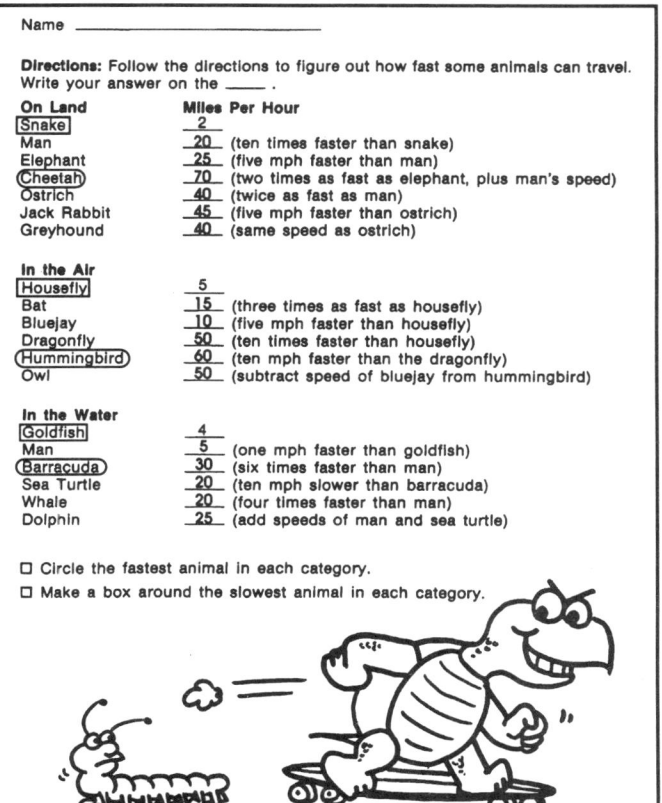

Page 73

Page 74

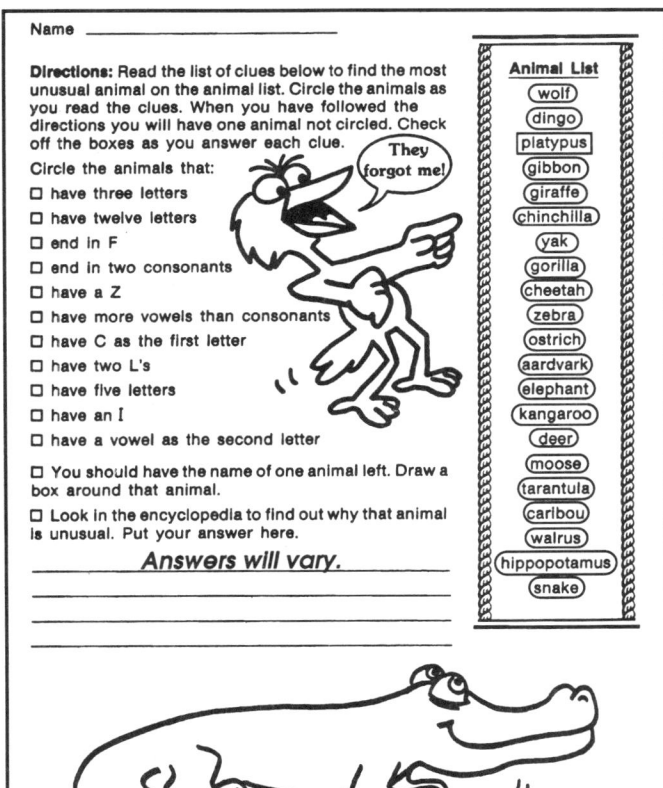

Page 75

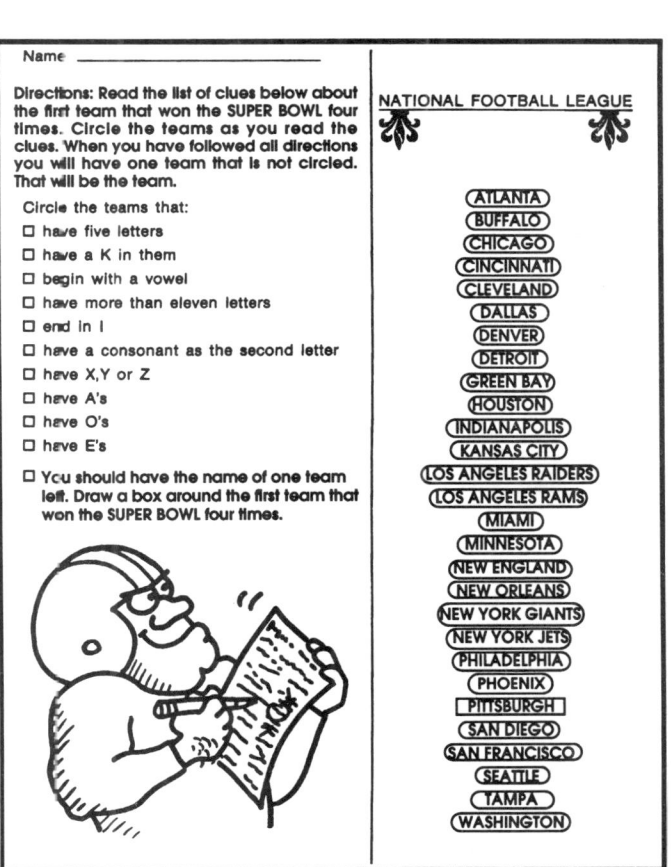

Page 76

Answer Key

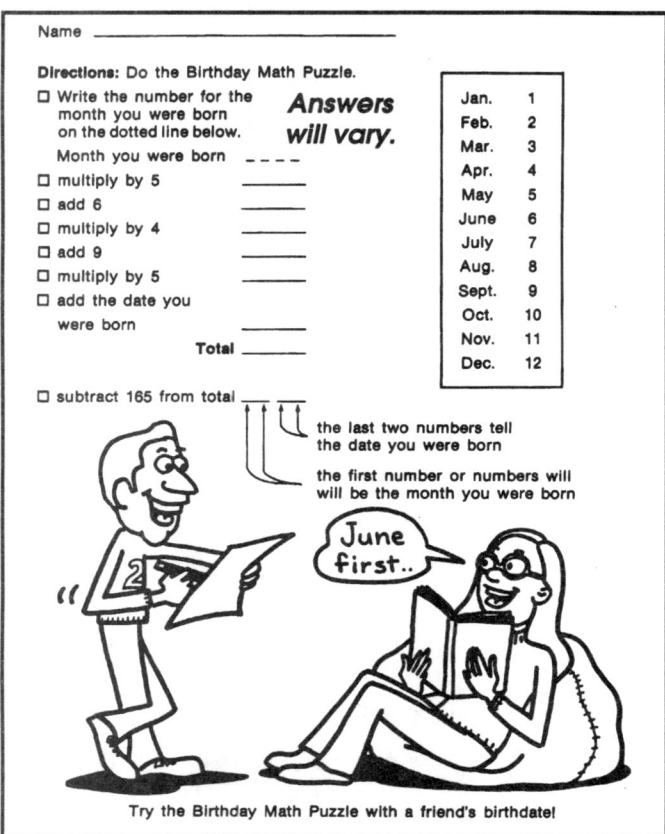

Page 77

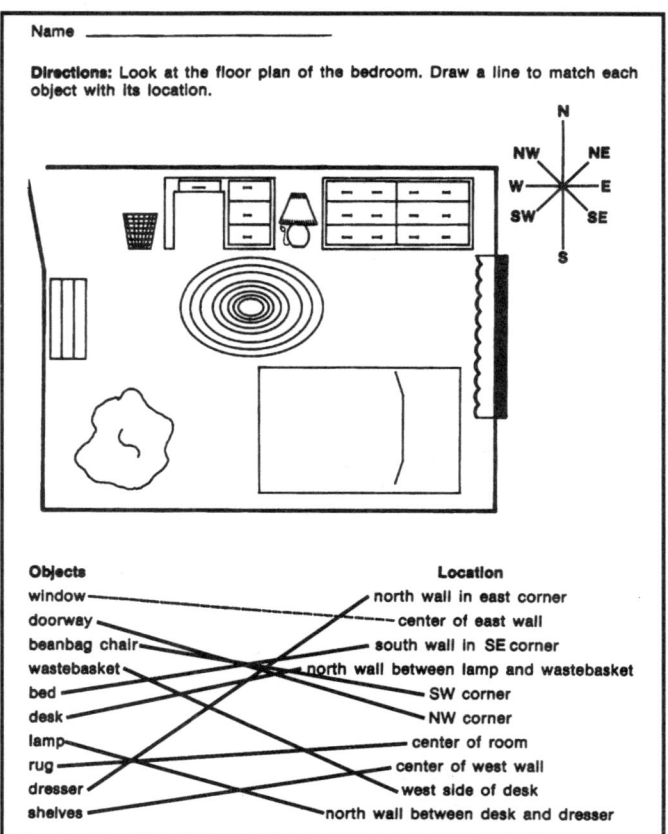

Page 78

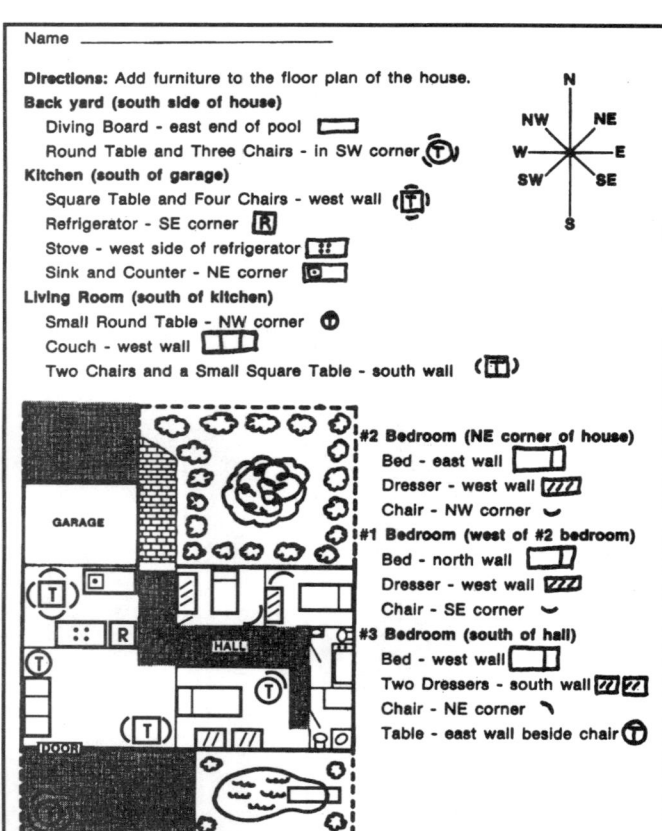

Page 79

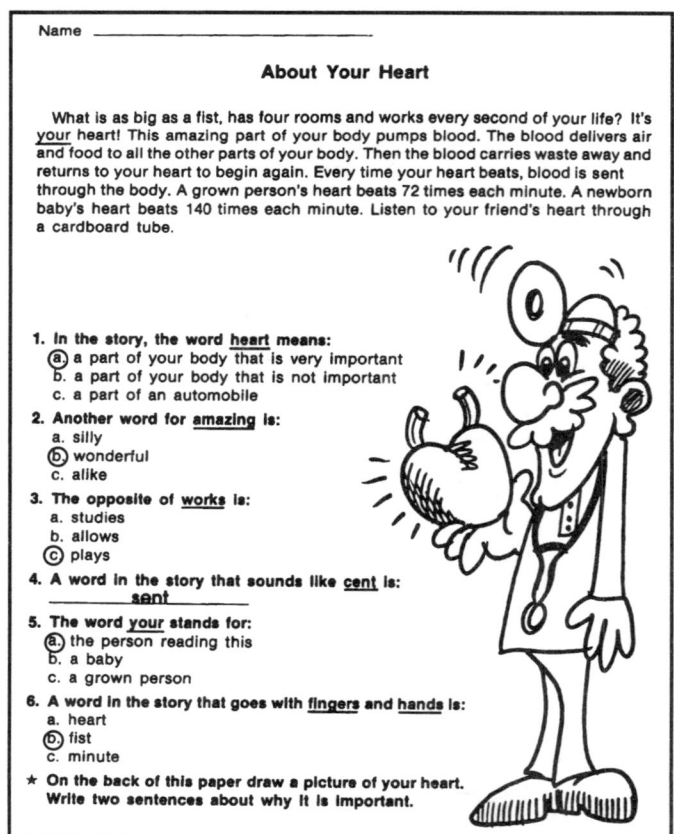

Page 80

Answer Key

Page 83

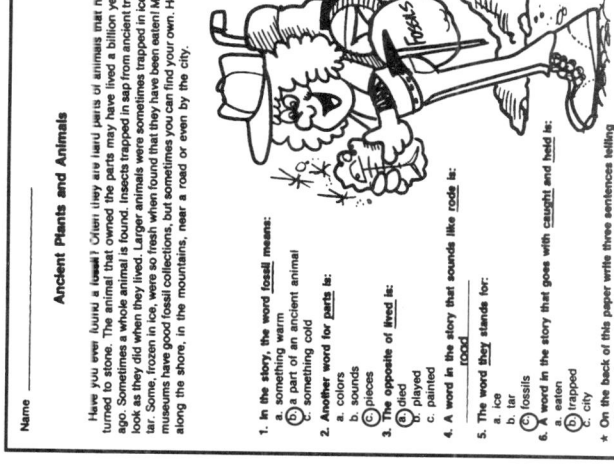

Page 86

Page 82

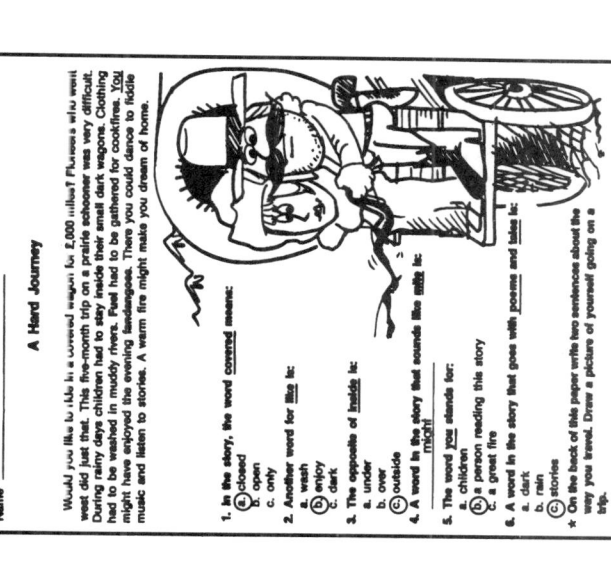

Page 85

Page 81

Page 84

Answer Key

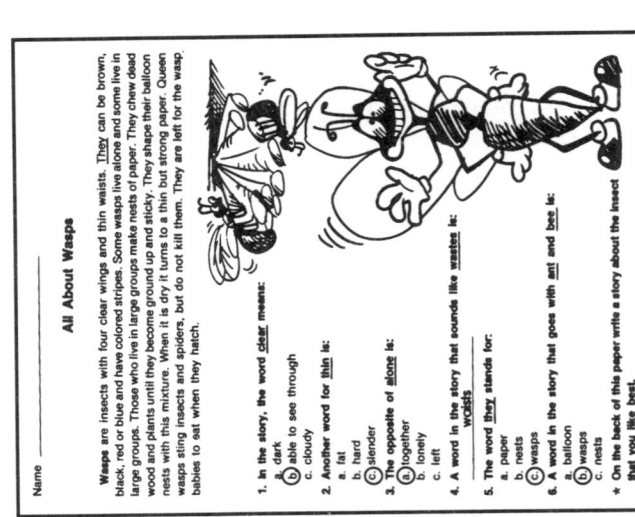

Answer Key

Page 93 — Mirror, Mirror On the Wall...

1. Who slept for twenty years?
   Rip Van Winkle
2. What do some ladies in Burma love?
   They love necklaces.
3. Where does the man with the beard live?
   in Norway
4. When did Mr. Din decide to grow his moustache?
   in 1949
5. Why don't Burmese women remove their necklaces?
   Their necks couldn't hold up their heads.
6. How long are Mr. Chalil's nails?
   100 inches long

Brainwork! Think about the question. Write the answer on the back. Make a list of all the bad and good things about having the world's longest nails.

Page 94 — The Long and the Short of It

1. Who was the world's tallest man?
   Robert Wadlow
2. What does Miss Tseng eat for breakfast?
   twenty dumplings
3. Where would a giant really stand out?
   in a crowd
4. When did Robert Wadlow die?
   1940
5. Why does Miss Tseng eat so much?
   She has a good appetite.
6. How do some dwarfs make a living?
   They are on TV or movies.

Brainwork! Think about the question and answer it on the back. Write a paragraph about why you'd rather be a giant or a dwarf.

Page 95 — Fabulous Food

1. Who thought he could eat a big hamburger?
   Gene
2. What contained 11,400 bananas?
   the world's biggest banana split
3. Where was the biggest burger made?
   in Australia
4. When was the biggest cherry pie made?
   May 15, 1976
5. Why was the cherry pie made?
   as part of a celebration
6. How was the biggest pizza served?
   in slices

Brainwork! Think about the question and answer it on the back. What "biggest in the world" food would you like to make? What would you do with it?

Page 96 — Champion Moneymakers

1. Who wanted to be a pianist?
   Linda
2. What game made Jimmy Connors famous?
   tennis
3. Where did Linda practice tennis?
   against the garage door
4. When did Sugar Ray lose his fight?
   in 1980
5. Why did Linda want to start taking piano lessons?
   to make more money
6. How did Fritz Kreisler make his living?
   He played the violin.

Brainwork! Think about the question and answer it on the back. Write a paragraph about what you want to be and why.

Page 97 — Super Sports

1. Who is the world's fastest bike rider?
   Dr. Allen Abbott
2. What did the American basketball team do in 1976?
   They regained their title.
3. Where do many great gymnasts live?
   in Eastern Europe
4. When did Eric Heiden win his gold medals?
   in 1980
5. Why does ice skating look hard to do?
   You skate on thin steel blades.
6. How could you beat Dr. Abbott's record?
   go faster than 140.5 miles per hour

Brainwork! Think about the question and answer it on the back. Write a paragraph telling how you think an Olympic athlete trains to win.

Page 98 — Speedy Sports

1. Who made a hockey puck go fastest?
   Bobby Hull
2. What is the world's fastest car race?
   the NASCAR
3. Where can you catch up on your sleep?
   at a wrestling match
4. When did William Yarborough go the fastest?
   in 1970
5. Why might someone like skydiving?
   It has speed and action.
6. Why is wrestling so slow?
   The holds can take a long time.

Brainwork! Think about the question and answer it on the back. Would you like to skydive? Write a paragraph telling why or why not.

Answer Key

Page 101 — Hard Work!
1. Who walked from Vienna to Paris? **Johann Hurlinger**
2. What difficult thing can Errol Bird do? **He can yodel.**
3. Where should you look for your old yo-yo? **In your closet**
4. When did yo-yos become popular? **In 1926**
5. Why was Johann's walk unusual? **He walked on his hands.**
6. How did Richard Baterip become Top Shiner? **He cleaned windows in the shortest time ever.**

Brainwork! Think about the question and answer it on the back. Which one of the stunts above do you think you could do best? Why?

Page 104 — Exciting Exercises
1. Who holds the record for push-ups? **Tommy Gildert**
2. What do you need to do lots of push-ups? **strong arms**
3. Where was the sit-up record set? **In California**
4. How long did William Vaught do twenty chin-ups? **In 1976**
5. How long did Mr. Suzuki jump rope? **9 hours and 46 minutes**
6. How can you start your sit-ups? **Lie down, put your hands behind your head and sit up.**

Brainwork! Think about the question and answer it on the back. How do you do your favorite exercise? Write directions so someone else can try it.

Page 100 — What Will They Do Next?
1. Who didn't drop their batons for 55 hours? **the Havant Hurricane girls**
2. What did Alison want to do? **break Wendy Wall's record**
3. Where did Barry Walls lie? **on a bed of nails**
4. When did the man in Sri Lanka stop clapping? **after 42 hours and 6 minutes**
5. Why did Barry Walls do his stunt in a store? **to draw people to it**
6. How do we often clap at a good performance? **like crazy**

Brainwork! Think about the question and answer it on the back. What kind of record would your mother like you to break?

Page 103 — Something to Sneeze About and Other Stories
1. Who was getting a cold? **Sam**
2. What was Marty having trouble doing? **falling asleep**
3. Where did the champion sneezer live? **In England**
4. How long did a woman yawn? **five weeks**
5. Why did Myra think Don was yawning? **She thought he was bored.**
6. How did the girl in England start sneezing? **She caught a cold.**

Brainwork! Think about the question and answer it on the back. Write about all the ways you know for stopping hiccups.

Page 99 — Can You Top This?
1. Who is a "one-man band"? **Rory Blackwell**
2. What unusual thing did Howard Davis do? **He let bees swarm on him.**
3. Where did Rory Blackwell live? **In England**
4. When could you try standing on one foot? **at recess**
5. Why didn't Howard die from bee stings? **The bees didn't sting him.**
6. How did Kathy peel her apple? **In one long peel**

Brainwork! Think about the question and answer it on the back. Why did it take Kathy so long to peel one apple?

Page 102 — Down on the Farm
1. Who eats the most cheese in the world? **the French**
2. What happens if feathers are left on a plucked chicken? **Everyone yells "Fowl!"**
3. Where might your wool sweater come from? **a sheep sheared by G. Phillips**
4. When did Mr. Phillips set his record? **on June 25, 1975**
5. Why was a "Cheese Mobile" necessary? **to move the biggest cheese wheel from Wisconsin to New York.**
6. How are most cows milked? **by machine**

Brainwork! Think about the question and answer it on the back. The word "fowl" is a homonym for "foul." Write the meanings of both words.